UNEXPLAINED

Judy Allen

KINGFISHER
BOSTON

KINGFISHER

a Houghton Mifflin Company imprint
222 Berkeley Street
Boston, Massachusetts 02116
www.houghtonmifflinbooks.com

First published in 2006
10 9 8 7 6 5 4 3 2 1

1TR/0606/SNPLFG/CLSN(CLSN)/140MA/C

Managing editor: Carron Brown
Coordinating editor: Stephanie Pliakas
Senior designer: Heidi Appleton
Picture research manager: Cee Weston-Baker
Senior production controller: Lindsey Scott
DTP manager: Nicky Studdart
DTP operator: Claire Cessford

Judy Allen's Web site:
www.judyallen.co.uk

The publisher cannot be held responsible for
changes in Web site addresses or content.

LIBRARY OF CONGRESS CATALOGING-IN-PUBLICATION DATA
Allen, Judy.
Unexplained/Judy Allen.—1st ed.
   p. cm.
Includes index.
ISBN-13: 978-0-7534-5950-8
ISBN-10: 0-7534-5950-7
1. Parapsychology—Encyclopedias,
Juvenile. 2. Curiosities and wonders—
Encyclopedias, Juvenile. I. Title.

BF1025.A38 2006
001.9403—dc22
2005032086

ISBN-13: 978-0-7534-5950-8
ISBN-10: 0-7534-5950-7

Printed in China

Contents

What is the Unexplained?

The unexplained takes many strange forms. It includes every mystery that has not been solved and every question that has not been answered. Are there ghosts? Can your dreams predict the future? Why do frogs fall out of the sky? What is the meaning of Stonehenge? Is the number 13 really unlucky? Where is Shangri-la? Is it possible for a groundhog to foretell the weather? Who makes crop circles? When will we find out if there are intelligent life-forms on other planets—and if they come to visit us?

With every year that passes, we discover and learn more, but we do not know everything yet. Of course, there are plenty of answers and solutions out there. They are in books, scientific journals, and popular magazines, programs on the radio and television, and specialized Web sites. Some are incomplete or unconvincing, and some contradict each other. Some, on the other hand, are absolutely correct—but which ones?

In this book you will find a few suggested explanations—the probable origins of some superstitions, the likely meaning of El Dorado, and a possible answer to the disappearances in the Bermuda Triangle. You will also find a great deal that remains unexplained.

*The world is such an extraordinary and
complicated place that it's very unlikely that
we will ever solve every puzzle, break every code,
and understand every awesome phenomenon. But
we can—and will—go on trying, and any one of
us may discover the key to something that has
been lost, hidden, or misunderstood
for thousands of years.*

Judy Allen

This photograph shows the empty library of Combermere Abbey, on the borders of Shropshire and Cheshire in England. It was taken in 1891. Not until the photograph was developed did anyone notice the ghost of the recently deceased Lord Combermere, sitting in his chair on the left.

CHAPTER ONE

HAUNTINGS

B y their nature, hauntings are difficult to define. Little is certain, except that there are different types of hauntings. Place memory is the replaying of a former event, while time slip brings the observer unexpectedly into the past. Poltergeists throw things and create noise and chaos. Then there are the others—the scariest of all—the unquiet spirits. These are the cause of shadows and ghosts, spooky atmospheres, and strange sounds. These are the truly unexplained.

HAUNTED HOUSES

Apparitions and strange atmospheres have been experienced in all types of places. They take many forms, from the friendly dead watching over the living to those who are mischievous, vengeful, evil, mysterious—or even imaginary. Three of the most famous stories concern an energetic poltergeist in Germany, phantom faces staring out of a floor in Spain, and a house built to appease restless spirits in California.

THE ROSENHEIM POLTERGEIST

In the late 1960s, strange things happened at a lawyer's office in Rosenheim, Germany. The telephones rang and then cut out when answered. Often the line went dead in midcall. Telephone engineers couldn't find anything wrong, nor could they explain why more than 600 calls were registered to the operator when no such calls had been made. Lights swung for no reason; fluorescent tubes and bulbs came unscrewed or exploded; pictures and furniture moved. Electricians, police officers, and physicists failed to find the cause. Then Professor Hans Bender of the Freiburg Institute for the Study of Parapsychology was called in. He knew that poltergeist activity is usually caused, unknowingly, by young people. He discovered the disruptive psychic energy was coming from an 18-year-old employee, Anne-Marie Schneider, who hated her job. Everything settled down when she left.

The anguished faces in the floor in Belmez could be chipped away or cemented over but always reappeared, sometimes aging and changing their expressions.

THE WINCHESTER MYSTERY HOUSE

Late in the 1800s, Mrs. Sarah Pardee Winchester came into a double inheritance—a fortune from the Winchester rifle company and a burden of guilt. When her husband died, a psychic told her that the spirits of those killed by the rifles could not rest. The only remedy was to build a house that was never to be finished. In 1884 she bought a farmhouse in San José, California, and employed teams of workers to follow her designs every day for 38 years, until her death. They created a vast, eccentric mansion, with 160 rooms, 40 staircases (some leading nowhere), 1,257 windows, and 467 doors (some opening onto walls). It is not certain if the house is haunted, though Sarah was convinced it was and often spoke to the ghosts.

THE BELMEZ FACES

Professor Bender was one of many investigators who failed to solve the chilling mystery of the faces that appeared in the floor of the Pereira family's house in Belmez, Spain, though he was certain that they were not a hoax. They were photographed and televised; sightseers lined up to see them; experiments were conducted. The entire floor was dug up—and human bones and two headless skeletons were unearthed. Even when these were given a Christian burial, the faces reappeared. Recording equipment picked up anguished cries, including "Justice!", "This hurts!", and "I want to go out." In 2004 the house was sold. The present state of the faces is unknown.

The architecture of Winchester house is eccentric, yet many features, including the heating and elevators, were ahead of their time. It is now open to tour groups—so visitors can make up their own minds whether or not it is haunted.

HAUNTED CASTLES

Castles and palaces have frequently been important to their country's history. Though palaces may stand in gentle estates, they were built to demonstrate royal power and in their day often seethed with intrigue. Castles stand for both royal and military power, and most have deep dungeons, once places of unimaginable suffering. Whether ghosts are unquiet spirits or echoes of the past, it is no surprise to find them in such potent surroundings.

THE TOWER OF LONDON

Beside the Thames river in London, England, stands the 11th-century Tower of London, probably one of the most haunted places on Earth. Its dungeons held thousands of prisoners, including kings, queens, and those accused of treason or heresy. Torture and execution were common. The aristocracy was beheaded on Tower Green, while commoners met their fate on Tower Hill, and their heads were stuck on spikes as warnings.

GHOSTS AT THE TOWER

It's no surprise that screams, weeping, and pacing footsteps are sometimes heard, and restless apparitions are occasionally seen. Sentries have reported stones thrown by no one; the shadow of a huge ax looming over Tower Green; headless figures—and, in 1815, a sentry collapsed and died after being menaced by the ghost of a brown bear.

For the first 600 years, the Tower of London housed the Courts of Justice, the Royal Observatory, the Royal Mint, and the first zoo in Great Britain.

VERSAILLES

Within the extensive grounds of the Palace of Versailles, just outside Paris, France, stands Le Petit Trianon—the setting of many disturbing apparitions. The earliest to be recorded were encountered in the late 1800s, and today they are still startling visitors.

Eleanor Jourdain and Charlotte Moberley gave a detailed description of their visions in their book *An Adventure*, published in 1911. The experiences of others have been similar. Many have seen a woman that they believe to be Marie Antoinette. Some have glimpsed workers in 18th-century clothes, and, perhaps strangest of all, they have noticed woodland and houses that have not existed for more than 200 years. It seems that the landscape as it was before the French Revolution returns to haunt the present— or is it that the observers slip briefly back to the past?

Le Petit Trianon was given to Marie Antoinette by her husband, King Louis XVI, in 1774.

Marie Antoinette (right) loved Le Petit Trianon (above). The rooms were furnished to her taste, and the grounds were landscaped as she directed.

Battlefield Ghosts

Ghostly scenes of conflict usually relate to ancient wars. This may be because today's targets can be bombarded from a distance, while in the past the entire struggle was concentrated on a single battlefield. Possibly the energy generated by rage, fear, and pain is the "electricity" that records the event on the landscape. Or maybe unfinished business leaves restless spirits behind, still striving to win a fight lost long ago.

Echoes in Dieppe

In August of 1951, a woman staying in Puys, near the French town of Dieppe, was woken up by the sound of explosions. They were so faint and far away that she went back to sleep and forgot about them. A few nights later, the woman and her sister-in-law, who was staying with her, were woken up by a tremendous uproar. They went onto their balcony and, though they could not see anything, clearly heard gunfire, men's voices shouting, the chilling noise of aircraft flying low and strafing the ground, and a series of blasts from heavy artillery.

Nothing at all had happened that night— but nine years earlier, on August 19, 1942, during World War II, Canadian, French, U.S., and British troops had launched a massive and disastrous raid on German forces in Dieppe, resulting in heavy casualties and little gain—a raid that would account for everything heard by the two women.

THE BATTLE OF CULLODEN

The last major battle on British soil was fought on April 16, 1746, on Drumossie moor (now called Culloden), near Inverness, Scotland. On one side were the Highlanders, led by Charles Stuart (Bonnie Prince Charlie). On the other—and hugely outnumbering them—were the English and Scottish troops led by the Duke of Cumberland. The defeat of the Highlanders marked the end of the Jacobite rebellion. The prince escaped, though few others did. Near the battlefield, the clash of swords and the screams of the dying have been heard, and the ghosts of marching Highlanders and blood-covered corpses have been glimpsed.

THE PHANTOMS OF FORT PULASKI

Fort Pulaski, near Savannah, Georgia, was the site of a one-sided Civil War battle in 1862. The Confederate troops thought that their fort was impenetrable, but the firepower of the attacking Federal forces proved them wrong. After 24 hours, the fort surrendered. If it had held out, many would have died, but surrendering with no fighting must have been difficult for the soldiers. That may be why so many soldiers seem unable to leave—the fort is still haunted by shadows and unexplained footsteps.

One Highlander's ghost still haunts Culloden. He is tall, with drawn features, and is said to whisper the word "defeated" when he is encountered.

Fort Pulaski, 1862

Ghosts on the Road

Driving alone along a deserted road at night—especially deep in the country where there are no lights—is always a little scary. But if something that is not quite human appears in front of the car or, worse, inside it, fear can turn into panic. Among the many frightening stories that have been told, one of the most frequent is that of the phantom hitchhiker.

PHANTOM HITCHHIKERS

They have been reported throughout Europe and the U.S.—hitchhikers who seem human—until suddenly they disappear.

Some of the tales are more convincing than others. If investigators are unable to trace the driver who picked up such a strange passenger and can only find people who have heard of someone it happened to, it may be a myth and not reality. But there are so many reports—can they all be false?

Typically, the driver stops to offer a ride to someone—often a girl who is alone. She gives an address and makes cheerful conversation until they are almost to her destination. When the car stops, she is silent, and when the driver turns to say good-bye—the car is empty. Sometimes inquiries at the chosen address are fruitless—but sometimes they have revealed that a girl of that description was killed on the road some years earlier.

Another shock experienced by unlucky drivers in Europe and the U.S. is a figure in old-fashioned clothes suddenly appearing on the road in the dark and vanishing underneath the car's wheels. But when the driver scrambles out to help, there is no one there.

18

VENGEFUL HANDS

In 1921 a motorcyclist crashed and was killed on a bleak road crossing Bodmin moor in Cornwall, England. No other vehicle was involved, and there was no obvious reason for the tragedy. Some years later, the driver of a four-door car crashed one night in the same desolate spot. He survived and described a pair of powerful, disembodied hands that seized the steering wheel and forced the car into a rocky ditch. There is no way of knowing if this is what happened to the motorcyclist—but other drivers since then have felt a sense of foreboding at the spot, and one or two have reported a brief struggle to regain control of the wheel from an unseen force.

In Norway, haunted places are marked by roadside signs, and people stop to visit them. This sign is posted on a road in Grotli, near the Jotunheim mountains.

THE MOTHMAN

Mothmen have been seen in the Russian Federation, the U.S., and the U.K., and legends of similar creatures occur in most countries of the world. They are rare, but terrifying. They seem to be very tall and completely gray, with humanlike bodies. Their faces are indistinct, but their eyes are a gleaming red. Witnesses say that they give out an aura of indescribable, bloodcurdling horror—then suddenly they unfold huge, leathery wings and take off, straight upward.

It is possible that some sightings have been of large birds—herons, eagles, owls with wide wingspans and silent flight—that are mistaken for something weird at dusk or by moonlight. But what were the others?

GHOSTS AT SEA

The Flying Dutchman *was the inspiration for*
Richard Wagner's opera Der Fliegende Hollander.

Phantom ships, manned by spectral crews, are said to ride the high seas, usually at night and often in foul weather. A few seem to be replaying their last voyages, before storms or rocks destroyed and sank them, forming a kind of visible echo. Some, though, are believed to be in the control of the vengeful wicked, who seek to bring misfortune and doom to any ship that acknowledges them.

THE FLYING DUTCHMAN

One phantom ship is more famous than any other. She is a 17th-century Dutch merchant vessel, a brigantine, traveling under full sail even when there is no wind and sometimes surrounded by an eerie light. According to legend, the ship got into difficulties trying to round the notoriously dangerous Cape of Good Hope off South Africa. Some say that her captain, Hendrick van der Decken, refused to seek the safety of a harbor; others say that he was prevented from doing so by the storm. Most agree that he swore a blasphemous oath that he would round the Cape if he had to sail till doomsday. And that, it seems, is what he is compelled to do. Sometimes he tries to pull up alongside other ships to hand over letters—but none who accept them survive. In fact, even to see the doomed ship is a bad omen.

Sightings have been recorded in the logs of many vessels. Keepers of the lighthouse at Cape Point have glimpsed the ship. Famous witnesses include British Prince George, later King George V; Nicholas Montserrat, the author of *The Cruel Sea* and *The Master Mariner*; and Captain Frederick Marryat, the author of *Children of the New Forest* and *The Phantom Ship*.

SHIP OF SKELETONS

The *Libera Nos* is another ghostly Dutch merchant vessel (below) that appears out of nowhere, under full sail. Everyone aboard, from the captain at the helm to the lookout in the crow's nest, is a skeleton. Like *The Flying Dutchman*, she is one of a number of "punishment ships," condemned to sail the oceans forever—or at least until her crew repents for their sins and offers prayers asking for forgiveness. *Libera Nos*, which means "liberate us," may be not so much a name as a desperate plea.

THE PALATINE LIGHTS

The Palatine lights, seen between Block Island and Rhode Island on the eastern seaboard of the U.S., flare brightly and then vanish into the sea—as though a ship has been consumed by fire and has sunk.

Controversy surrounds the haunting. In 1738 a ship carrying immigrants from the Palatinate (as the Rhineland in Germany was called at the time) was wrecked on the island. What happened next is in dispute. Some say that the passengers were rescued; others believe that they were murdered by the islanders, who then burned the ship.

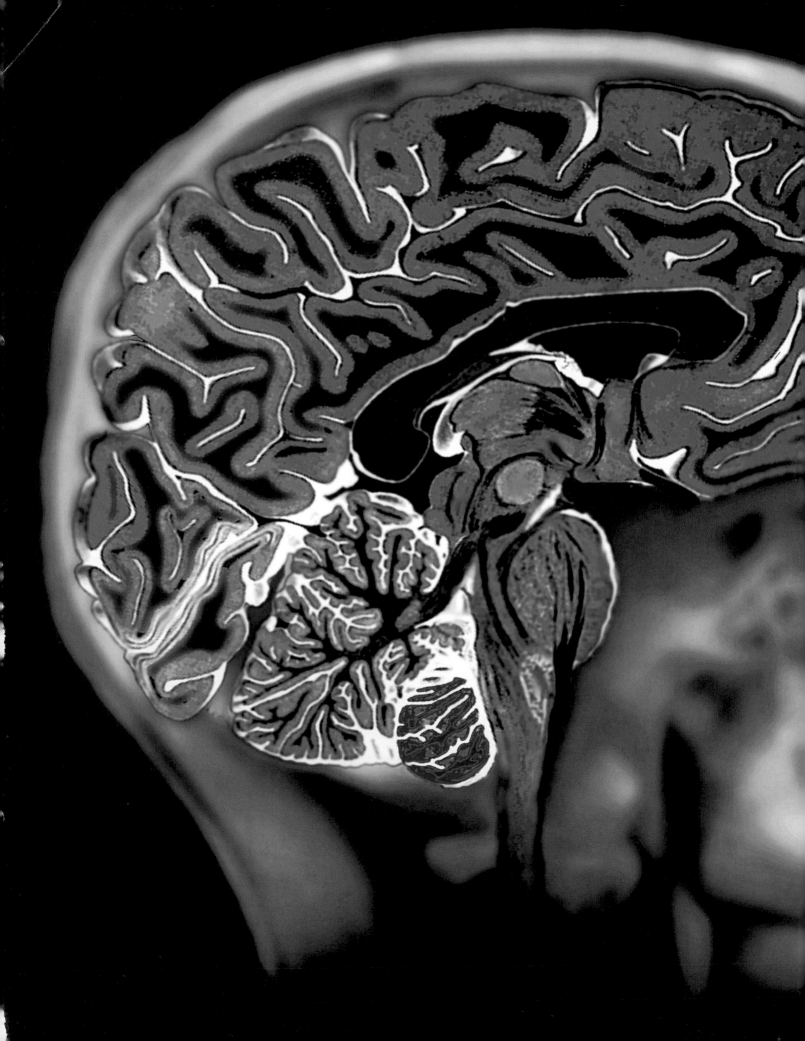

Chapter two

The power of the mind

The conscious mind and its abilities are largely understood. The unconscious mind, however, remains full of mysteries, even though individuals and scientific institutions constantly study and experiment to learn more about its powers. It almost seems to work on its own, with little help from the conscious mind or the body. It may solve problems during sleep, show glimpses of the future, perhaps predict things that have not yet happened, or even manipulate physical objects.

When we sleep and the conscious mind is at rest, the unconscious mind continues to work as a dream maker and a problem solver.

Sixth Sense

The best-known senses are sight, hearing, smell, taste, and touch. Then there is that mysterious sixth sense, sometimes called ESP—or extrasensory perception. Do our brains have extraordinary abilities that science has not yet explained? Is the number of senses greater than five? Or do our five senses pick up more than we realize—subtle scents, chemical signals, and sounds at the very edges of our range?

ESP

It is widely agreed that ESP exists. By its nature, however, it is not easy to study. The term covers phenomena in which someone receives information without apparently using any of the five known senses. It includes telepathy and foretelling the future.

Sometimes, though, the sixth sense can be physical. It is thought that an area in the nose may be able to pick up on Earth's electromagnetic field. This could be the source of our sense of direction (definitely stronger in some people than others).

It is possible that, like other animals, we can detect vibrations traveling through Earth and changes in air pressure. The brain processes these signals, whether or not it can make sense of them. An enormous amount is known about the brain's complex workings, but there is a lot still to discover. Despite studies using fMRI scans (right), we are nowhere close to developing a computer that can read minds.

This fMRI (functional magnetic resonance imaging) scan shows that the area in the right side of the brain, responsible for moving the left hand, is active. Because different areas are used to look at faces and objects, scans can also show which of two pictures someone is seeing.

Déjà vu

"Déjà vu" is French for "already seen," although it actually feels more like "I have been here before." It is unlike normal memory. Realizing halfway through a movie that you have already seen it is not déjà vu. It is something much stranger—a feeling that you have experienced something before, while knowing that you have not. Perhaps surprisingly, déjà vu usually strikes at very ordinary and undramatic times. Is it, as some say, because we have lived this life before? Or could it be that the unconscious mind registers the moment a microsecond before the conscious mind so that, when it reaches the conscious mind, it is perceived as a memory?

Telepathy

Telepathy is the transfer of ideas and images directly from one mind to another, sometimes over great distances. Tribal societies regard it as normal. Scientific societies consider it special, something only for psychics and mystics. It is easy to be suspicious of telepathy because magicians can fake it. Certainly a great deal has yet to be explained. Many people report having "known" that someone they care about is sick or in danger, long before news arrived in a more conventional way. People may also experience thinking about a friend just before that friend calls or stops by.

Experiments in which two people try to "send and receive" the simple images on Zener cards have not succeeded often enough to convince those who disbelieve.

Psychic Detectives

C rystals and cards, mystics and oracles, shamans and witches—all have been used to solve crimes. Today there are sophisticated techniques, including DNA matching and computers to check information. Even so, there is still a place for those with the old skills, under a different name. Many doubt their powers, but the police still pay cautious attention to them. They are known as the psychic detectives.

Blue sense

It is called blue sense after the color of most police uniforms, and it is something that many experienced police officers have. It is often called "a hunch." An officer may feel certain that a witness is lying, even when there is no apparent reason to think so. It may inspire an officer to pursue an inquiry in a new direction; to apply for a warrant to search a house that seems only indirectly connected to a crime; to insist on questioning someone again; or to be aware of danger before it is obvious. It may be that some people are more observant and better at picking up signals. Or perhaps the mysterious—and still unexplained—sixth sense really is at work.

Sir Arthur Conan Doyle's famous detective, Sherlock Holmes, was a fictional example of the value of blue sense—his intuition seemed almost paranormal, until he explained the clues that he had discovered.

THE MISSING GUITAR PLAYER

One piece of successful psychic detection took place in 1974. A valuable painting, *The Guitar Player* by Jan Vermeer (1632–1675), was taken from the Kenwood House museum in London, England, in a smash-and-grab raid. A psychic named Nella Jones had such a strong vision of the location of the stolen picture that she contacted the police. She told them that the thieves had taken off the heavy frame and dumped it. The police were polite but dismissive— until they found the frame where she had said that it would be. They called her to the site, where she found the metal alarm that had also been removed. They were so amazed that they regarded her as a suspect until thorough checks ruled this out. Thanks to her, the picture was recovered undamaged.

Nella Jones (below) correctly predicted that a ransom would be demanded for Vermeer's The Guitar Player *(above) and then guided police to the cemetery where it was hidden.*

TRUE OR FALSE?

Most police forces pay some attention to psychic detectives; a few take individual psychics seriously. Yet it is probable that the majority disbelieve. One problem is that there are thousands of people who mistakenly believe that they have these abilities, and it takes time to sift these out. Another problem is that it is not always easy for a genuine psychic to interpret his or her thoughts and visions. Finally, no one yet knows how it all works. If ever the psychic mechanism is understood and can be developed and used at will, no crime will ever go undetected again.

Dreams and Premonitions

*S*ome people believe that dreams foretell the future or that they show the dreamer's hopes and fears. Others think that the sleeping mind uses symbols to guide or to warn—a donkey means that you are being stubborn, a dragonfly that things are about to change, and a birthday cake that your wishes will come true. It is also said that dreams symbolize opposites—dream that you are crying, and you will be happy soon.

The assassination of Archduke Francis Ferdinand of Austria and his wife in 1914 led to the outbreak of World War I (1914–1918). The event was foreseen in a dream, but there was neither the time nor the opportunity to prevent it.

PREDICTING THE FUTURE

Even if a disaster is foreseen, it cannot necessarily be avoided. In 1980 psychic Alex Tanous said that a famous rock star would die young and in an unusual way. Soon afterward the famous singer John Lennon was shot dead outside his New York City apartment building.

On June 28, 1914, Monseigneur Joseph de Lanyi, the bishop of Grosswarden in the Balkans, dreamed that he received a letter from his former student Archduke Francis Ferdinand of Austria. It said that the archduke and his wife had been assassinated. Disturbed, the bishop prayed for them. Later a telegram arrived with news that the couple had been shot.

PROBLEM SOLVING

In 1865 a German chemist, Friedrich August Kekule (1829–1896), tried to figure out the structure of the molecules of benzene (a colorless and dangerous chemical). He fell asleep thinking about the atoms that make up each molecule. In a vivid dream, the atoms twisted in front of his eyes and became an ouroboros, a snake catching hold of its own tail. When he woke up, he knew that he had solved the problem while he was sleeping—the atoms in a benzene molecule really do form a circle.

The ouroboros (right) is an ancient symbol used by alchemists, the first chemists. In a dream, it solved the mystery of the structure of the benzene molecule (below).

CREATIVE DREAMS

Some of Charles Dickens' (1812–1870) characters first introduced themselves to him in dreams. Robert Louis Stevenson (1850–1894) could dream whole chapters and then would write them down the next day. One of his best-known books is *The Strange Case of Dr. Jekyll and Mr. Hyde*. In the book Dr. Jekyll discovers a way of separating the good and bad in his own nature. Stevenson puzzled for some time over how the doctor would achieve this. Then he dreamed the now famous moment when the doctor mixes and drinks the concoction that turns him into the hideous and evil Mr. Hyde.

Robert Louis Stevenson (right), the author of many books, including Kidnapped *and* Treasure Island, *dreamed a crucial scene for* The Strange Case of Dr. Jekyll *(above, left) and* Mr. Hyde *(above, right).*

Mind and Matter

Is it possible to make things happen just by the power of thought? Many believe that it is. The process is called psychokinesis (PK), meaning "psychic movement." It can take many forms, including levitation (see pages 32–33) and poltergeist activity (see page 12). Causing objects to bend or move just by concentrating is PK in action. Experiments seem to show that it is easier to redirect a moving object—like a thrown ball—than it is to move something that is still.

BENDING AND TWISTING

One extraordinary example of PK energy is the apparent ability to bend metal. An object, usually a spoon or a fork, twists out of shape after being gently stroked, even though physical force is not used. Uri Geller is probably the best-known spoon bender. He has been challenged by the magician James Randi, who says he can do the same thing by sleight of hand and trickery. However, Geller also claims that he can use mind power in other ways, including to stop or start watches and clocks—even if the watch is in front of a television screen when his program is on. This ability has yet to be proved or explained, but it never ceases to fascinate.

Mónica Nieto Tejada, a 15-year-old Spanish girl, successfully bending a metal strip inside a sealed glass container, using PK in 1989.

MOVING AND SHAKING

Can someone move an object without touching it? Or control how a pair of dice falls? Experiments in many countries have produced mixed results, but studies continue. This psychokinetic energy can be spontaneous or planned. Spontaneous PK, possibly resulting in poltergeist activity, is hard to test scientifically—not that it is easy to test planned PK either. It may be that, although it is being used consciously, the unconscious is somehow involved—and the unconscious does not respond well to laboratory conditions. (Of course, this argument does not impress scientists.)

Perhaps everyone has PK power without knowing it. Possibly those healers who cure by simply laying their hands on a patient have learned to put it to good use.

PHOTOGRAPHING AURAS

There is an ancient belief that each person is surrounded by an aura. Auras are usually invisible, though some people seem able to see—or sense—them. They are said to vary in color and strength, and there is a theory that they can be used to diagnose a patient's spiritual or physical health.

In the 1940s, Seymon Kirlian, a Russian electrician, developed a method of photographing auras. He connected a source of electrical power to a plate holding photographic film. The subject—a hand, perhaps, or a leaf—was placed on the film, and a high-frequency, low-voltage charge passed through it, with dramatic results.

Kirlian photographs show the natural electrical output of living things—a body, a hand, a leaf. And a human subject can sometimes make the effect stronger at will. But is this really the aura spoken of by mystics and mediums?

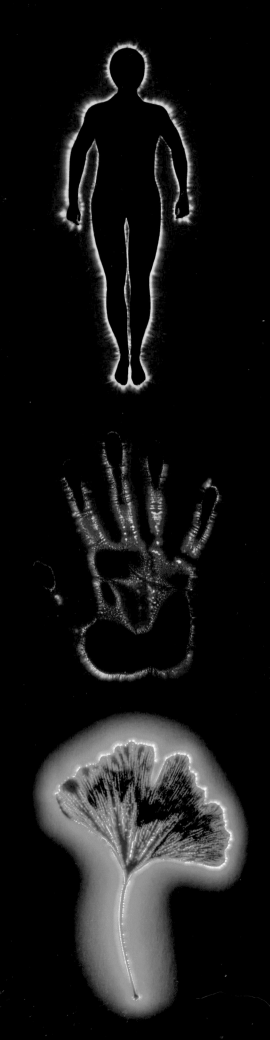

Levitation

"To levitate" means to rise and float in the air—unusual behavior for people or objects. To rise without support means defeating the laws of gravity. Many say that this is impossible without trickery of some kind. Yet, for thousands of years, holy men and women—Buddhists, Muslims, Christians, shamans, and other mystics—seem to have achieved it, and psychics have given demonstrations that have yet to be explained.

SPIRITUAL STATES

In the 1500s, St. Teresa of Avila wrote in her autobiography that in moments of religious ecstasy she was unable to prevent herself from rising off the ground. She tried to resist out of humility, not wanting to seem different to the other nuns of her order.

In the 1600s, St. Joseph of Cupertino levitated frequently and involuntarily, once in the presence of Pope Urban VIII.

In each of these cases and that of Subbayah Pullavar (left) and also of Daniel Dunglas Home (opposite), it was clear to observers that the central figure was in a powerfully altered spiritual state.

In southern India in 1936, a British tea planter, P. T. Plunkett, photographed Subbayah Pullavar in a trance and levitating horizontally above the ground. Plunkett was carrying a walking stick and was able to move it above, below, and all around the yogi. This convinced him that there were no hidden supports.

THE FAMOUS MR. HOME

Daniel Dunglas Home (1833–1886) was
one of the most famous spiritualist
mediums and levitators. Well-known in
the U.S. and Europe, he performed for
Emperor Napoléon III, the king of Prussia,
and the czar of Russia. Not that he met with
approval everywhere—in 1864, he was
banished from Rome, Italy, accused of sorcery.

He was thoroughly investigated, not only by
skeptics and scientists but also by conjurors
and stage magicians. It seems that he was
able to lift tables, chairs—and himself.
Once, in a well-lit room in front of
witnesses, he rose in the air and
floated out of a third-floor window
and in again at the next window.
No one found any signs of fraud.

MAGNETIC LEVITATION

Magnetic levitation is achieved when
a strong magnetic force defeats gravity.
Items can be lifted if opposing magnets
of sufficient strength are placed where
they will change the magnetic field
around them. So far, scientists have
levitated coins and pieces of crystal.
More is clearly possible, because
China's Maglev trains
run on a cushion of
air held in place by
powerful opposing magnets.

Why is it unlucky to walk underneath a ladder?
Could it be because it severs the connection
between the head, which contains the
spirit or soul, and heaven? Or is it
because whoever has climbed up
the ladder could drop something?

CHAPTER THREE

SUPERSTITIONS AND SYMBOLS

The world is big and often frightening. Superstitions are supposed to make it safer, to bring good luck, or to avoid something bad. However, it is not likely that seeing a black cat or spilling salt can affect the future. Yet, in every country and every culture, there are hundreds, perhaps thousands, of these beliefs. At worrying times—on dangerous journeys or before exams—even people who are not superstitious are tempted to touch wood or to carry a lucky charm.

FEAR OF NUMBERS

Ⅱumbers are magical, as well as being useful. Individuals and entire cultures believe in their power for good or evil. Number 1 is perfect because it cannot be divided. Number 3 is usually lucky, especially if three wishes are granted. Number 4 should be avoided in China, Japan, and North and South Korea. In most of the rest of the world 13—although formed of two fortunate numbers—is the unluckiest number of all.

The tarot is a set of early playing cards, used for games and fortune telling. The 13th card is Death. However, this rarely means human death; it usually stands for change, including change for the better.

UNLUCKY DINING

The earliest and probably best known of the "13" superstitions is that it is unlucky for 13 people to sit down to eat dinner together. If they do, one will die within the year. Another guest must be found, or, as a last resort, a stuffed animal should be seated in the 14th place. No one knows where this idea began. The usual explanation is that there were 13 people at the Last Supper (below), after which Judas betrayed Jesus to those who crucified him. Yet Jesus and his 12 disciples met on many other occasions, and also the superstition did not appear until the 1800s, almost 2,000 years later.

APOLLO 13

The number 13 featured prominently in NASA's third attempt to land men on the Moon—and not only in the spacecraft's name. *Apollo 13* was launched at 13:13 P.M. on April 11, 1970. The explosion in *Apollo 13*'s oxygen tank, which ended the mission, happened on April 13. Despite this, *Apollo 13* made it safely back to Earth with its three-man crew—so perhaps 13 was not so unlucky after all.

FATAL FOUR

In China, Japan, North and South Korea, and Taiwan, the taboo number is 4, but the reason for this is simple—the word for "4" sounds like the word for death. In these countries license plates are not issued with a 4 in the sequence, and the numbers of apartments and houses often jump from 3 to 5. The same is true in other countries with large Chinese populations—such as Toronto in Canada.

FRIDAY THE 13TH

Friday was the execution day in ancient Rome—the day on which Jesus of Nazareth was crucified. It was also Hangman's Day in medieval Great Britain. This may be why Friday the 13th is seen as an especially unlucky day.

Friday is named for the Norse Freya, a fertility goddess whose chariot was often drawn by black cats. Christianity suggested that she was a witch. This may have added to the fear of Friday—although, for many, it is a holy day. Friday is the day that Muslims go to the mosque, and the Jewish Sabbath starts on Friday.

BEYOND 12

The number 12 is said to be complete, whole, and perfect. There are 12 signs of the zodiac; 12 months in the year; 12 hours in the day and 12 in the night; there are 12 tribes of Israel and 12 disciples in the Bible; 12 gods in Norse mythology and 12 Greek gods on Mount Olympus. Perhaps 13 arouses suspicion and dread because it goes beyond the perfect 12 into unknown and possibly dangerous territory.

In Indonesia, on the other hand, 12 is an unlucky number; in Italy, 17 is unlucky; and in China, 13 is lucky because it sounds like the words for "must succeed."

37

THE POTENCY OF COLORS

The gift of a red envelope, with good-luck symbols outside and money inside, is traditional during Chinese New Year.

The symbolism of colors is ancient and complex. Red stands for both love and violence. Green is associated with vegetation and life or decay and jealousy. Blue may represent calmness and spirituality or coldness and defeat. Black can suggest evil and death, but it is also the color of fertile soil and the sacred stone of Islam. As the symbolism varies, so do the superstitions, and one person's unlucky color is believed to be fortunate by another.

Some say that green is the color chosen by fairies and that they will punish humans who use it.

38

THE POWER OF RED

Red is almost always seen as a positive, energetic color. It is the color of blood and therefore of life. In many cultures, from Native American to Chinese, it is a lucky color, bringing happiness, success, and wealth. It features strongly in Chinese New Year celebrations. However, red is also the color of Mars, the red planet, which is ruled by the Roman god of war, who also gave his name to the month of March and the word "martial."

UNLUCKY GREEN

Green is the color of nature and immortality and appears on many national flags. So why is it considered unlucky throughout the U.K. and U.S.?

The earliest record of this superstition is from the late 1700s and warns that wearing green brings death. In 1778 a Swedish chemist, Carl Wilhelm Scheele (1742–1786), experimented with a mineral substance called arsenic. He created a new color that he called Scheele's Green, which became fashionable for wallpapers and fabrics. Scheele knew that arsenic was highly poisonous, but, as he did not expect people to eat their clothes or furniture, he did not think that it mattered. However, if it becomes damp, Scheele's Green gives off a poisonous gas. Significant numbers of people became sick or even died from it. Arsenic greens finally disappeared by the early 1900s— but perhaps some memory of this toxic color lingers on.

CONTRADICTORY YELLOW

Yellow is the color of the sun and so of life. Imperial yellow once belonged solely to the emperors of China. Novice Buddhist monks wear white and then yellow before they become teachers and wear orange. Yet, in some cultures, yellow stands for cowardice and also for sickness and death, symbolized by a leaf turning yellow before it dies and falls from the tree.

This is the death mask of the French emperor Napoléon Bonaparte (1769–1821), who died on the rainy island of St. Helena. The cause of his death was cancer, but there were rumors of poisoning. A lock of his hair was analyzed in 1960 and was found to contain arsenic. In 1980 an analysis of his wallpaper showed that it contained Scheele's Green.

THE SIGNIFICANCE OF SALT

There is one mineral that is more valuable than any other. No magician could create a substance with more properties. It is essential to life. It has 14,000 known uses, including preserving, healing, fertilizing, cleaning, and making medicines, dyes, cheeses, and plastics. Roads were built to transport it. Wars were fought over it. It dissolves in water, but when the water evaporates, it reappears. It is called sodium chloride—better known as salt.

Ancient Egyptians used natron, a mineral salt containing sodium chloride, to prevent mummified bodies from decaying.

PRECIOUS TRADE

The Phoenicians were the first to trade in salt. It was prized by the ancient Egyptians, who used it in mummification. The ancient Greeks called it a divine substance. The ancient Romans paid their workers in salt money, called a "salarium," the origin of the word "salary."

Because it never changes and will reform even if it is dissolved in water, it is compared to the unchanging love of God and is used in religious rites and ceremonies.

SALT OF THE EARTH

Salt is found in the rocks of the earth. Deposits may appear aboveground, as salt mountains (below), or lie deep underground so that mines must be dug to reach them. Over time, some is liquefied by rain and carried to the sea by rivers. There, salt pans built in the shallows allow the sun to burn off the water, leaving salt crystals behind.

In a cavern 650 ft. (200m) below the ground, these figures carved from solid salt have survived hundreds of years in a salt mine in Wieliczka, Poland.

SALTY SUPERSTITIONS

Salt is a substance that has attracted many superstitions. Traditionally, it brings prosperity and so is given to people in the new year or when they move into a new house. It also brings fertility and is given to a bride on her wedding day. But, mostly, salt brings protection. It seems to be a natural step from knowing that salt can preserve the bodies of the dead and protect foods from decay to believing that it also protects against evil. Salt is regarded as a defense against witchcraft and against curses delivered by the evil eye. It is considered very unlucky to spill salt. Some people say that this is because it is valuable and should not be wasted. Others say that spilled salt awakens demons—the antidote is to throw a pinch over the left shoulder (below) in order to banish the evil spirits who, as folklore tells us, tend to gather there.

41

Wood, mirrors, and iron

It is very important to keep a horseshoe the right way up, or otherwise the luck drains out of it and is lost.

Certain materials are believed to carry the power to grant good fortune, to protect, or to bring harm. Wood, mirrors, and iron are three of the best known of these. One of the most widespread superstitions is that of touching—or knocking on—wood. Broken mirror glass is commonly thought to cause seven years of bad luck. An iron horseshoe is a popular good-luck charm.

SACRED TREES

"Touch wood" usually follows a positive statement—such as: "Everything's going well—touch wood." Sometimes this is accompanied by the speaker actually touching wood. It is often difficult to find the origin of any superstition, but there are two main possibilities for this one.

Firstly, it may symbolize touching the wooden cross on which Jesus of Nazareth was crucified, thereby seeking religious protection.

Secondly, it was sparked from a fear that an evil spirit might overhear, suspect the speaker of boasting, and decide to make everything go wrong by way of punishing him or her. Most ancient civilizations believed in sacred trees inhabited by deities who had power over human fate. Perhaps, originally, it was important to touch a specific tree. Or perhaps it was necessary to knock on any nearby tree while speaking so that the resident spirit could not hear the words (right).

METAL FROM HEAVEN

It is likely that the first
iron discovered by humankind
was found in meteorites (right),
which were known to have dropped
from heaven above. This is probably why
iron was believed to have supernatural
qualities and to be a good defense against
evil, including vampires and werewolves.
It is possible that horseshoes are lucky not
only because they are made of iron but also
because the horse was a sacred beast in several
cultures. To be truly lucky, though, a horseshoe
must be found, not bought or accepted as a gift.

MIRROR OF THE SOUL

Mirrors have always had magical associations. They are
portals, allowing access into other worlds. Also, they
show an image of the soul of the person who is looking
into them. The first mirrors were still pools of water,
where ripples could splinter the reflection. Next came
highly polished metal, which was hard to break and gave
a constant reflection. When glass mirrors were developed
in 7 B.C., the reflection was again in danger of being
shattered. If mirror glass is broken while someone is
reflected in it, the person's soul breaks too and
is said to take seven years to heal. This is
why seven years' bad luck supposedly
follows such a disaster. This is an old
superstition that may have been
strengthened because glass was
very expensive in its early days.

*Shattered mirrors could
be unlucky because broken
glass is sharp and dangerous.*

43

JEWELS OF FATE AND FORTUNE

Jewels are said to have special powers. This may be because it is difficult and sometimes dangerous to collect them from deep inside the earth or under the sea or because they are always beautiful, usually valuable, and sometimes rare. Whatever the reason, it is said that they can protect, warn of danger, or bring luck—either good or bad.

Early in the 1900s, a rumor spread that the blue Hope diamond was cursed. Its last private owner, Evalyn Walsh McLean (above), said that unlucky jewels were lucky to her. She—and her dog (who often wore it on his collar)—survived the curse.

Opals can be milky white or vivid green, but they always have rainbow flashes of light. At one time it was believed that opals came down from the sky through lightning.

OPALS

Opals were once prized as the luckiest of all gemstones. Sadly, in the 1800s, they became known as stones of ill omen. It was said that King Alfonso XII of Spain (1857–1885) gave an opal to his wife, who died within months, and that later owners of the stone, including the king himself, died soon after wearing it. This, however, occurred during the time when many people died young because of the disease cholera. It was also noticed that opals glowed until the wearer died—when they lost their fire. It is now known that opals react to body temperature.

BIRTHSTONES

There are alternatives, but below are the best-known birthstones. January has the red garnet, which protects travelers, and February has the purple amethyst, said to guard against drunkeness. For March, there is the pale blue aquamarine of the sea goddesses. April has the diamond, which looks like a pebble until it is cut and polished. May has the emerald, and June has the alexandrite (named for Czar Alexander II) or the pearl, once worn only by royalty. For July, there is the ruby, a talisman against evil. August has the peridot, once called "gem of the sun," and September has the sapphire. For October, the opal; for November, yellow topaz; and for December, the turquoise, imported from Turkey.

In 1849 the Koh-i-Noor was presented to Queen Victoria of England. Women seem immune to its reputed bad luck, and it is now in the front of the crown that was worn by Queen Elizabeth, the Queen Mother (1900–2002).

THE KOH-I-NOOR DIAMOND

There is no doubt that this lustrous diamond came from India, but its earliest owners are unknown. Some say that it belonged to the god Krishna himself and then to the first Mogul ruler of India, Sultan Babur (1483–1530), and Shah Jahan (1592–1666), who built the Taj Mahal. The diamond was named, so the story goes, by Nadir Shah (1688–1747) of Persia (now Iran) who took it from the turban of Muhammad Shah (1702–1748), the last Mogul ruler, when he defeated him in battle (right). Seeing it, he cried, "Koh-i-Noor," meaning "mountain of light." Many of its later owners were imprisoned or exiled, and the stone was blamed for their misfortunes.

WHERE JEWELS ARE FOUND

A diamond is the hardest natural substance in the world. Indian diamonds were often found in riverbeds, but in South Africa some mines were dug very deep. Emerald mines are not deep in the ground but are open workings on the surface. A pearl is made when a piece of grit gets inside an oyster, and the oyster grows a substance around it to stop the irritation.

THE POWER OF NAMES AND TALISMANS

A name is more than just a word. It contains some of the essence of whoever or whatever it stands for. Holy names should be spoken with respect; the names of demons with caution. Naming children is seen as important all over the world, and there are usually ceremonies for this. A name can carry as much power as a talisman. In fact, a name can be used as a talisman.

ankh   *hammer of Thor*

TALISMANS

A talisman contains an active force, whereas an amulet is more passive and protective. While an amulet can shield against a curse or the evil eye, a talisman can bring positive benefits—or so it is said. The Egyptian ankh, in the shape of a cross with a loop at the top, stands for long life and fertility. The Scandinavian hammer of Thor promises strength and success. In China, the dragon is for luck, prosperity, and life-giving rain. The heart is a universal symbol of peace and love.

A SECRET NAME

In a well-known German fairy tale (right), a father pretends that his daughter can spin straw into gold, and she is held captive in the castle by a king, who awaits this wonderful transformation. A magical dwarf, Rumpelstiltskin, appears and carries out the task for her, but in exchange he demands her firstborn child. She and the king get married, and soon they have a baby. She begs the dwarf to release her from her promise, and he agrees—but only if she can guess his name within three days. At the last moment, a servant overhears the triumphant dwarf singing his name—and the baby is saved.

NAMES AND COINCIDENCES

In 1898 a short novel was published—
The Wreck of the Titan by Morgan Robertson.
In it, the fictional ocean liner *Titan* hits an
iceberg in the North Atlantic Ocean and sinks,
with many people killed. In 1912 a real liner,
Titanic, struck an iceberg in the North Atlantic
and sank, also with great loss of life. Many
details of the ship and accident are the same.
Two less dramatic incidents followed in 1935.
First, a cargo vessel, *Titanican*, became trapped
in pack ice in the North Atlantic and had to be
freed by an icebreaker. Then a passenger
steamer, *The Titan*, collided with a dock in
Hamburg, Germany. Coincidence? Probably.
Something in the name? Who can say . . .

The sinking of the Titanic *is one of
the most famous of all disasters at sea.*

CALLING OUT NAMES

The names "fairy" and "fairies" should be
avoided. Call them The Little People or
The Good Neighbors. It is also said to be
unwise to speak of The Furies, the three
fateful sisters of Greek mythology. Call them
The Kindly Ones instead, in the hope that
this is what they will be. The names of
humans should be used with care too.
Deliberately mispronouncing someone's
name is an insult. A cruel nickname can
be damaging, while an affectionate
one brings warmth and love.

CURSES AND JINXES

The idea that it is rude to point or stare is an echo of an ancient warning. Pointing is often an essential part of giving a curse. A fixed stare could be delivering something known in most countries and still feared in many—the evil eye. This can be deflected by a mirror, a polished shield, or an image of a single eye. Protection from curses and jinxes is more complicated.

The Chamsah, an open hand, is an amulet used to ward off the evil eye and is also a good luck charm.

THE CURSE OF TUTANKHAMEN'S TOMB

The tomb of the young Egyptian king Tutankhamen (c. 1341–1323 B.C.) remained undiscovered until 1922, when it was opened by Howard Carter, an English archaeologist, and the Fifth Earl of Carnarvon, who funded the expedition. Both were overwhelmed by the splendor of its contents. Soon afterward Carnarvon died from a mosquito bite. Rumors of a curse grew as more people connected with the excavation died, apparently in mysterious circumstances. Howard Carter never believed in the curse, but the powerful mythology of ancient Egypt—and the guilt at the desecration of the grave—kept the story alive.

POINTING THE BONE

The belief that an object can be filled with dangerous power is not uncommon. Among the Aborigines of Australia, bone pointing, a type of ritual murder, is well-known. The weapon, loaded with magical force, may be made out of a human or kangaroo bone or even wood or stone. It is ceremonially pointed at the victim, accompanied by chanting, and, unless the spell is lifted, death follows. The cause of death may be the victim's own fear, which causes the abandonment of hope and a refusal to eat or drink.

Howard Carter (kneeling) and A. R. Callender, who discovered the stone sarcophagus, open Tutankhamen's tomb in 1922.

THE SCOTTISH PLAY

Theater is a superstitious world. Many actors carry good-luck charms and avoid whistling in their dressing rooms or wearing green. Before a traditional Japanese play, salt is scattered on the stage in order to ward off evil spirits. But the most famous superstition hovers like a dark cloud around William Shakespeare's tragedy *Macbeth*. There are numerous stories of accidents and disasters falling on those involved in productions of the play—especially if the title is spoken or lines are quoted offstage. But there have also been many occasions when nothing at all has gone wrong.

The three witches—and the spell they chant—are thought to be responsible for any curse on the play Macbeth. *It is said that the spell is real, capable of calling up dark forces.*

A JINXED CAR?

In 1955 the movie star James Dean (1931–1955) crashed his silver Porsche and died instantly. The original accident was almost certainly the result of speeding, but afterward the car seemed to be jinxed. First it slipped off the breakdown truck and injured a mechanic. Then it was dismantled, and the undamaged parts were reused. The car with the engine killed its driver; the cars with the crankshaft and the tires injured theirs. Finally, the wrecked body of the Porsche managed to injure one person and later kill another one when it fell from the back of a transporter.

BIRDS OF ILL OMEN

Birds are significant in most cultures. There are probably more superstitions about them than there are feathers in the world. Their ability to fly seems somehow magical. They rise to heaven, perhaps transporting souls, and return, maybe with messages from the gods. Birds of ill omen are often all white or all black, though the black-and-white magpie and the brilliantly colored peacock have their share of stories.

THE CRY OF THE PEACOCK

The peacock, originally from southern Asia, has a magnificent tail and a screech that is loud enough to wake the dead. It is a sacred bird in Hindu mythology, associated with Indra, the god of thunder, and is said to dance when the rains come. In Chinese mythology, it symbolizes dignity and beauty. In Christian art, it stood for the resurrection of Jesus because its tail feathers molt, fall off, and then regrow.

In Asia, the peacock is a sacred bird, but in Europe, it has its dark side. There, the "eyes" on its tail were said by some to signify the evil eye and its call to warn of impending doom.

THE CALL OF THE OWL

The owl is a bird of the night, often associated with death, mourning, and evil. In many countries, it is linked to witches and sorcerers, who may use it in their spells or may even disguise themselves as owls. Though often considered evil, the owl was also used as a protection against dark forces. However, in fantasies and fairy tales owls are often benevolent and wise, and they were well loved in Greek mythology— the owl belonged to the goddess of wisdom, Athena, and was the emblem of Athens.

THE OMINOUS MAGPIE

In China, the magpie is a bringer of good fortune, and terrible bad luck will fall on anyone who kills it. In Europe, it is also unlucky to kill one, but this is more surprising, because the magpie, so they say, is the devil's bird. To see a lone magpie is very unlucky. To see a group of them is worrying because they are probably plotting something evil. A pair of magpies, though, is a good sign, and a single magpie sitting on a roof protects the house.

Magpies are thieves that love bright things such as jewelry and tinfoil.

THE IMPORTANCE OF RAVENS

The night-black raven, with its cruel beak and glittering eyes, is widely regarded as an omen of death. Even more frightening were the Turnfalken, supernatural ravens that haunted the Habsburgs, who, for centuries, were the most powerful dynasty in Europe. The Turnfalken warned of (or perhaps caused) death and disaster. The story goes that, in the A.D. 1000s, ravens saved a Habsburg ancestor from a flock of vultures that would have killed him. In gratitude, the Habsburg built a watchtower in the forest, called it Habichtsburg (hawk's castle), fed the ravens, and encouraged them to live there. One hundred years later, his heirs turned it into a vast castle—Schloss Habsburg—and drove away or killed the ravens. Not surprisingly, they took revenge. The Turnfalken were seen at every Habsburg defeat in battle, just before Marie Antoinette (a Habsburg) was led to the guillotine, and before Archduke Francis Ferdinand and his wife visited Sarajevo (now part of Bosnia) in 1914, where they were both assassinated.

Symbolic Animals

*S*ymbolic meaning is attached to both real and mythical animals. This idea is ancient and widespread, though the qualities that each animal represents vary from culture to culture. The Western dragon is generally evil, and the Eastern dragon is usually benevolent. In African stories, the lion may be the king of beasts—or foolish and easily tricked. Of the thousands of symbolic animals, the horse, hare, and dog are among the best known.

The magnificent eight-legged horse Sleipnir was the steed of Odin, the greatest of the Norse gods.

The dog

The domestic dog belongs to the same family as wolves, hyenas, and foxes. Perhaps this is why its symbolism is contradictory. On the dark side, the devil was thought to take the form of a black dog, and Cerberus, the guardian of the gates of the underworld in Greek mythology, was a ferocious three-headed dog. Traditionally, dogs are clairvoyant. They can sense the presence of ghosts, they howl when a death in the family is near, and they know instinctively if a stranger can be trusted or not. However, the dog also stands for faithfulness and loyalty. Sirius, the Dog Star, the brightest star in the sky, follows steadfastly at the heels of his master, the constellation of Orion, the hunter.

Coats of arms

Heraldry began simply, with symbols on shields and banners so that armies could recognize their own soldiers. Later it developed complex rules and meanings, with many groups, including aristocratic families and cities, having their own coats of arms. The reason for the use of particular colors, designs, or animals is often obscure, except in the "canting" coats of arms. These use visual puns, so "Baring" has a picture of a bear with a ring through its nose, and "Harthill" has a hart— a male deer—standing on a mound.

THE HORSE

Horses symbolize power and
wealth, speed, and strength. In many
myths horses pull the Sun across the
heavens and sometimes the Moon, too.
They were created by the Greek sea god,
Poseidon (called Neptune by the Romans),
and "white horses" can be seen on the tops of
storm-whipped waves. They share with dogs the
ability to sense the presence of ghosts, and there are
stories of horses becoming ghosts themselves. They have
few negative aspects, though the mythical creatures of the
North, the water horses, can be dangerous, and no one wants
to see the horses that take part in the Wild Hunt with the devil
and his pack of red-eyed hounds.

THE HARE

Strangely, since the hare is such a timid creature, it
has a sinister reputation in some mythologies, which
believe it to be evil—the familiar of a witch or the
witch him or herself in disguise. Throughout medieval
Europe, a hare crossing a person's path was bad luck,
yet the foot of a hare or rabbit brought good luck. In
pre-Christian Europe, it symbolized fertility. To some
of the First Nation Native American tribes, it was the
creator of the universe. In China, it was associated with
the Moon. In ancient Greece, the same belief was held,
which brings the hare full circle since a Greek moon
goddess, Hecate, was the queen of the witches.

*The hare has bulging eyes, an
eerie cry, and a habit of standing
upright to look for danger. Is this
why it was thought to be a
witch in animal form?*

THE LORE OF CATS

Do cats bring good or bad luck? Today opinions differ. Yet in most of the world, for most of the time, cats have been loved and honored. Thai legends tell of cats guarding temples; in Japan, in A.D. 999, the palace kittens were treated like princes; Prophet Muhammad of Islam cut off the sleeve of his robe rather than disturb his sleeping cat. Only in medieval Europe was the cat regarded as evil.

THE SACRED CAT

For thousands of years, humankind's greatest enemies were neither wolves nor snakes but were the mice that ate food supplies and carried diseases. The early Egyptians noticed wild cats hunting mice and encouraged and tamed them. They saw that as well as killing mice and snakes, they were beautiful and were good mothers. In homes, they were loved. In temples, they were worshipped as sacred creatures. At first, they belonged to the sun god. Later they were associated with goddesses and the moon. Like the moon, their eyes shine in the dark, and their pupils can change from round-to crescent-shaped.

Cats kept their special place within Greek, Roman, and Norse mythology as these beliefs spread. Bastet, of Egypt; the Greek and Roman moon goddesses, Artemis and Diana; and the Norse Freya, whose chariot was drawn by two black cats, were all fierce huntresses who also protected women, especially mothers, and children. This might seem to be a contradiction—until you consider the nature of the cat.

Killing a cat in ancient Egypt was punishable by death because it was believed that Bastet, an Egyptian goddess (right), sometimes inhabited their bodies. When cats died, they were often ceremonially mummified.

ANCIENT ANCESTORS

The cat's earliest lynxlike ancestors evolved around 34 million years ago. Around 4,000 years ago, the ancient Egyptians began taming small wildcats. Every domestic cat's ancestors originated in Egypt; the Greeks transported them to Europe, and from there they traveled by ship to most countries of the world.

DEVIL CATS

In 13th-century Europe, everything changed. Pope Gregory declared that black cats belonged to Satan, the devil, and soon cats were linked with witches (above). Some believed that they were "familiars," who carried messages between their witch and Satan, and could work some of the witch's evil spells themselves; others thought that witches were shape-shifters who sometimes took the form of cats. This began the idea that a cat could bring bad luck.

BLACK AND WHITE

Superstitions surround cats. There are too many to list, but the idea that it is either lucky or unlucky for a cat to cross a person's path is widespread. Black cats are lucky in some places, including the U.K., Australia, and parts of North America, and white cats are unlucky. In other parts of North America and many European countries, it is the other way around. In the Russian Federation, blue cats are lucky, and in France, it is especially lucky to find a black cat with one white hair. It is said that a black cat in the house will ensure that a sailor or fisherman comes home safely.

It is always lucky to have a cat on board a boat or a ship, but it is unlucky to mention its name.

The Magic of Trees and Flowers

Trees and flowers are important to us in so many ways. On the practical level, they provide food and fuel and medicine, and they are used for making buildings, clothes, musical instruments, perfumes, gardens, and wind shelters. On another level, though, they vibrate with symbolic meanings and magical powers. Almost every culture has its own sacred tree and special flowers, and those who understand this have passed their knowledge down through the generations.

In Norse mythology, Yggdrasil, the World Tree, is a giant ash. This artist's colorful representation of the tree shows the fiery underworld and a rainbow of life in the branches.

THE TREE OF LIFE

Look up at any tall tree, and you will understand why so many people believe in a Tree of Life, with its roots in the underworld, its trunk passing through the home of humans and animals, and its branches reaching up to the sky. In ancient Egypt, it was the sycamore. To the Greeks, Romans, Hebrews, and throughout northern Europe, it is usually the oak, though in Norse mythology it is the ash. In the Middle East, the great tree is the cedar and in the Far East, the bo, or pipal (fig), tree. All are sacred, respected not as gods but as powerful channels, or links, between heaven and earth, reminding us of our place—halfway between what is above and what is below.

Lakshmi, the Hindu goddess of wealth, light, and fortune, is often shown seated on a lotus flower. It is a symbol of her spiritual power.

THE ELDER TREE

Of all the magical trees, the elder tree is one of the strangest and most contradictory. In the depths of the winter, its twisted, dark branches look menacing, yet in the spring it is full of white blossoms. Most parts of it are poisonous and evil-smelling, yet it is used in medicine, and its flowers and berries make good wine. It belongs to witches and fairies, yet it can offer protection from them and their familiars and curses. It must never be cut down, nor its wood burned, and even lightning, it is believed, will not ignite it. Tradition says that before taking any part of the elder for use, its permission should be requested.

Naturally, the giant sunflower is a symbol of the Sun, revered by the Incas of Peru as an image of the sun god. Among the tribes of the plains in North America, sunflower seeds were given to the dead as food for their journeys to the afterlife.

FLOWER POWER

Many flowers have healing properties. Even more carry symbolic meanings. The lotus, a type of water lily, is the greatest of all. It flowers in the Near and Far East and from North Africa to the Americas. The lotus has become a symbol of resurrection and purity and of the Sun, which rises daily from the darkness, because its lovely bloom grows from the sludge at the bottom of ponds.

The Moon has many flowers dedicated to it, including *lunaria*, whose name comes from "lunar," Latin for "moon." It grows in Europe and Central Asia. It has purple flowers whose silvery seed cases gleam like pale moons—often called honesty. It is said to have the power to ward off evil spirits and bring wealth.

Feng shui

Feng shui means "wind and water." It is an ancient Chinese system of placing everything—buildings, landscapes, furniture—in harmony with the natural energy of the universe. It is the science of allowing this chi, or energy, to flow freely, with its paths unblocked. There are many pronunciations. In mainland China, it is something like "foong shway." In Hong Kong, it is more like "fun soo-ee." The West uses "feng shoe-ee."

The mysterious science

The science of feng shui is complex and practical. In its earliest days, it was a secret knowledge, used to benefit only the emperor and the most powerful in the land. As the centuries passed, it has become widely known and used, especially in the Far East. Correctly applied, it promises to increase energy, happiness, and success. Yet the lines of chi are as silent and invisible within the landscape as within the human body. A feng shui practitioner will discover them in various ways, often using a compass. In fact, the earliest compasses were developed in China for this purpose, in the 2nd century B.C., though they were not used for navigation in Europe for hundreds of years, until the end of the A.D. 1100s.

Straight lines

Chi should meander gently. Straight roads, paths, and lines let it travel too fast and become destructive. If a straight path leads to a door, the chi can be deflected and softened by a mirror hung above the door frame.

The feng-shui compass, or lo pan, is set in a square base so that it can align with a wall or door for an exact reading of the direction that a building faces.

The resting places of ancestors

The earliest application of feng shui was in the positioning of graves. Every aspect of the landscape would be taken into account and also the birth and death dates of the deceased. This is seen as possibly the most important function of all. Every person has a line of ancestors, stretching back into the distant past. Even if he or she knows nothing about them, they still existed—just as, for many, a line of descendents will lead into the future. If the ancestors are respected and their burial sites are chosen and placed correctly, the benefits will follow through the generations.

GREEN DRAGON AND WHITE TIGER

There are many calculations to consider when constructing a building, designing a garden, or reorganizing a house or room. The five directions—north, south, east, west, and center—must also be considered. So, too, must the five Chinese elements—water, fire, earth, wood, and metal—and the five symbolic creatures that belong to them. The center is earth, represented by the yellow phoenix. The east is wood, the green dragon. The west is metal, the white tiger. The south is fire, the red bird, and the north is water, the black turtle. It is also necessary to consider yin and yang—usually understood as female and male, darkness and light. These two exist in everything, and what matters is to keep them in the right balance.

The lines of chi are called lung mei, or dragon paths.

The Aurora Borealis (northern lights) and the Aurora Australis (southern lights) are caused when electrically charged particles from the Sun react with Earth's atmosphere.

Chapter four
Natural Phenomena

Most people know that this is a world where extreme weather can strike—droughts and floods; earthquakes and volcanoes; thunder and lightning; hurricanes and tornadoes; blizzards and hail; and cold harsh that is enough to freeze the earth, rivers, and seas.

Not everyone knows that it is also a world in which stones can move by themselves, statues cry, humans burst into flames for no apparent reason, and frogs and peaches drop out of the sky.

Fire and Light

The world is full of fire and light—but not only from the Sun, Moon, and stars. Meteors, burning up in the atmosphere, become shooting stars. Storms send lightning from cloud to cloud and cloud to land and create sprites and elves (tiny bright flashes in the air). The auroras wave shimmering streamers. And there are other, more mysterious, effects.

BALL LIGHTNING

Scientists agree that ball lightning is real, but they cannot agree what it actually is. It only appears when the air is charged with electricity during—or just after—a thunderstorm, but it is very different from normal lightning. It looks like a floating, glowing sphere, which can be any color and as small as a baseball or as large as a basketball. No one who has seen it will ever forget it.

The impact of the Tunguska fireball, which was recorded by seismographs in the U.S. and Java, Indonesia, caused gale-force winds in Russia and kept the skies bright throughout Europe until after midnight.

TUNGUSKA

Meteors usually burn up in the atmosphere or fall harmlessly into the ocean. But, in late June, our planet passes through a collection of space debris known as the Beta Taurid stream, thought to be the remains of a disintegrating comet. In June 1908 an enormous fireball was seen shooting across the sky over Tunguska in Siberia. It exploded before it hit the ground, starting a catastrophic forest fire. In 1927 a scientific expedition found signs of a massive explosion and fire—but no crater. Was it Beta Taurid debris— or, as some say, the crash landing of a UFO?

Ball lightning drifts through the air, passing easily through walls and then vanishing within around ten seconds—sometimes silently, sometimes with a sharp explosion.

SPONTANEOUS HUMAN COMBUSTION

Reports of spontaneous human combustion began in the 1600s and continue today. There are stories throughout the U.K., across North America, and in places as far apart as India and Hungary, France and Singapore, Antigua and Germany. In most cases, the person burst into flames for no discoverable reason and was burned almost completely. This rare and dramatic death has been written into many novels, including Charles Dickens' *Bleak House.*

There is no confirmed scientific explanation, but here is one of many theories. Every human body contains varying strengths of electrical fields (which is why it is possible to get a mild shock from metal). Every living body also contains gases—oxygen in the lungs and methane in the intestines. Electrical charges can ignite these gases.

Photographs of spontaneous combustion are too gruesome to print here. This digitally created picture shows how some surrounding material— and even shoes—can remain untouched.

SOME FACTS AND FIGURES

Satellites and space shuttles tell that us there are around 1.4 billion lightning flashes worldwide every year (around 44 per second).

Sprites and elves are also called TLEs, or Transient Luminous Events. They are caused by gas molecules in the air being activated by the electricity in a storm.

There are two major meteor showers visible from Earth—the Perseids in August and the less predictable Leonids in November.

Sound and Movement

Sounds are vibrations that move through the air.
Movements can be caused by sound, though
there are many other causes too. We think we know
what sound and movement are, but the laws of physics
cannot always explain them. Among Earth's mysteries
are unaccountable loud, booming sounds in the air,
strange cries that have no known origin,
and stones that seem to move by themselves.

The power of sound

In Tibet, there are rumors of monks whose
chanting can create antigravity and raise
stones above the ground (left). This ties in
with a long-held theory that the huge stone
blocks of some great structures of ancient
times were raised into place by the power
of sound. Neither story impresses
scientists—and yet . . . more and more
researchers are suggesting that sound
played an important role in the ceremonies
at Neolithic stone circles and tombs.
Acoustic physics (the study of the physical
effects of sound) shows that drumming or
chanting could create a resonance, or
vibration, in these places that would be
very dramatic. Also, physicists have
succeeded, in laboratory conditions, in
defying gravity and raising a heavy sphere
of tungsten by using ultrasound waves.

THE MOVING STONES OF DEATH VALLEY

Death Valley National Park in California is hot,
arid, and mountainous, with extraordinary rock
formations, numerous disused mines, and a dry lake
bed, known as Racetrack Playa. The surface of the
Playa is mud, baked hard by the sun, and scattered
over it are stones—some as small as pebbles,
others as large as boulders. And these stones
move, leaving clear tracks on the ground.
No one has ever seen it happen, but charts
of the stones' positions show that it does—
and that some can travel up to 197 ft.
(60m), leaving looping, twisting trails
that may even backtrack on themselves.
How they move is a mystery. It is not
gravity, because the ground is flat.
Possibly the night dew makes the
surface slippery, and the wind pushes
them—but why do they sometimes
move on windless days? Possibly
there is a magnetic force under
the ground—but why, when
three rocks are lying together,
will two move in opposite
directions, while the third stays
in the same place for months?

*According to the laws of physics, it is not possible
for bumblebees to fly. Their bodies are too heavy for
the size of their wings and the speed at which they
flap. Fortunately, bumblebees do not know this!*

FROG SHOWERS AND FISH FALLS

It is common knowledge that weather descends from above—rain, hail, snow, and even lightning. It is startling that pieces of metal can tumble from an aircraft and also from satellites and space probes. It is amazing that several tons of meteorites, mostly very small, land on the planet daily. But some falls are completely astonishing.

The occasional fish, berry, or twig can slip from a bird's beak, but most falls involve much more than one bird could carry.

STRANGE RAINS

Sea creatures cannot drop from the sky—or can they? In A.D. 200 Athanaeus, a Greek historian, was the first of many to record a heavy rain of fish. In the 1500s Bergen, in Norway, was deluged with dead mice; live maggots showered onto Acapulco, in Mexico, in the 1900s; and downpours of frogs have been noted in numerous places in most centuries. It is not only animals that can rain down. In 1957 thousands of 1,000 franc notes fluttered onto the French town of Bourges; in 1961 Louisiana was pelted with green peaches; in 1969 golf balls rattled onto Florida; in 1987 southwest England was drenched in red rain (Sahara desert sand from Africa)—then, in 2004, it was fish again, splattering down onto Wales.

Tornadoes are formed when warm air, which rises, meets cold air, which descends. This causes a narrow, powerful tube of spiraling wind, often called a twister.

THEORIES AND EXPLANATIONS

Simple mistakes can be made. In Alaska, lemmings are called "sky mice" because, in the spring, their tracks begin to appear in areas of unmarked snow. They do not drop from above, though—after waking from hibernation, the lemmings burrow up from below. Not all explanations work so well. Frogs like wet weather, so they might be seen on the ground when it rains, but after a frog rain, they are found on roofs. The idea that strong winds lift and carry things could explain the red rain and the annual shower of live sardines in Honduras at the start of the stormy season. Yet winds were not recorded before many of these events, and how could winds collect hundreds of frogs but no pondweed, snails, or mud?

ANGEL HAIR AND MARSH PAPER

The first record of falling "marsh paper" was in the Balkans in 1687. A piece like a sticky black tablecloth was saved and, when analyzed, found to be made of algae and tiny water creatures clumped together. No one can analyze the pale, silky threads of "Angel Hair," often tangled, which have been reported in Canada, France, and England, because it disappears soon after landing. Some say that it is the threads used by young spiders to travel to new areas; others say that it is from the exhausts of UFOs. Until it is explained, all is a mystery.

CELESTIAL CYCLES

Earth is a sphere that turns and travels through space. Millions of stars, suns, planets, moons, comets, asteroids, and grains of space dust surround us—some near, some far. The Sun that we belong to and the Moon that orbits our planet have cycles and seasons that affect life on Earth.

The eight planets of the solar system affect our lives on Earth as they travel through space.

COMETS AND ASTEROIDS

We have named and tracked them, but there are things that we do not know about these space travelers. The paths of comets are long. They may not reappear for many years, but they can be predicted. Traditionally, it is believed that they signal major events and the births of great leaders.

Asteroids are huge chunks of rocks. If one collided with Earth, there would be a massive explosion and a dust cloud that could block out sunlight for years. It is possible that the dinosaurs were destroyed by such an impact. However, if an asteroid was trapped by Earth's field of gravity, we might have a second moon!

The zodiac (right) is a belt encircling Earth, around which the Sun, Moon, and planets pass. It is divided into 12 signs, named after patterns of stars (constellations), and is used to calculate the effect of the heavens on human lives.

THE TURNING OF THE YEAR

The Sun is essential to life. As Earth spins, the Sun seems to move across the sky, causing night and day. As Earth travels through space, the Sun seems to pull closer for a while and then pull away again, causing the seasons to change. It has always been important to track these seasons—to know when to plow, when to plant, and when to harvest. Fear of losing the Sun has inspired many ceremonies and sacrifices, including human sacrifices, that are designed to strengthen it after its winter months of weakness.

MOON POWER

The Moon seems alive, changing shape as it waxes, or grows, into a full circle, and then waning, or shrinking, to a crescent shape. It has many powers—some magical, some real, and some uncertain. It is said that a full Moon is a witch's moon and a time for werewolves and madness. (The word "lunatic" comes from the Latin *luna*, meaning "moon.") The pull of the Moon causes the tides, and many believe that it has control over plant life—seeds should be planted just before a full Moon; plants harvested when the Moon is waning; fruit picked at full Moon to eat and stored at new Moon.

Statves and Stone

The word "petrify" has two meanings—to paralyze with fear or to turn to stone. Stories from ancient Greece and Rome warn that one look from the snake-haired Gorgon Medusa or the reptilian basilisk would petrify someone in both senses of the word. It may seem unlikely that a person could ever become a statue in this way—yet many people believe that there are statues that behave like people.

A desert traveler who is unfortunate enough to look a basilisk in the eye is petrified in both senses of the word.

WEEPING STATUES

A statue can be quite disconcerting. With a little imagination or the action of flickering candlelight, it can appear to move its limbs or eyes. But a statue that weeps tears (or even blood) is not so easily explained. There are reports of such things from the U.S., Mexico, and Puerto Rico and from Europe, Australia, and Africa. Once a statue cried on a specific occasion. A Pennsylvanian man owned a bronze head and shoulders of a Japanese girl. Tears ran from its eyes on August 6, 1945, the day that an atomic bomb was dropped on Hiroshima. It is possible that some weeping statues are fakes, and condensation, liquefying paint, or melting glue could account for others. Many, though, have been carefully examined, and no scientific reason has been found. For these, the mystery remains.

Statues of the Virgin Mary, such as this one in Porto San Stefano, Italy, may seem to cry tears of blood.

The Dropping Well in Yorkshire, England. Some of the objects left to petrify can be seen hanging in the dripping water.

PETRIFYING WATER

Objects may not be able to experience fear, but they can be petrified—even without the stony stare of Medusa or the basilisk. In Knaresborough—in Yorkshire, England—there is an extraordinary well. It is located next to the cave where the renowned witch Mother Shipton was born in 1488. It is said that she foretold many events, including the Great Fire of London in 1666, and that she set plagues of goblins on her enemies. Her cave and the well have been attracting visitors since the 1600s. The well water rises from an underground lake, collecting minerals from the rocks that it travels through. As the water pours down the natural wall behind the well, it slowly builds up new layers. Objects left hanging in the flowing water turn to stone. The curators at the well say that a stuffed animal will be rocklike within three or four months.

Komodo dragons are monitor lizards from Indonesia and can grow up to 10 ft. (3m) long. They are dangerous, and although there are several in zoos around the world, none has ever been tamed.

CHAPTER FIVE
STRANGE CREATURES

At one time stories were told of ferocious, flesh-eating dragons. They were said to have teeth like knives, snakes' tongues, and poisonous saliva. Most believed that they were mythical. Then, in 1912, creatures exactly like this were discovered on the Indonesian island of Komodo. Stories are still told of strange, unknown animals living in other remote areas of the world. Perhaps one day they, too, will be tracked down and brought out of mythology and into reality.

Water Monsters

The surface of the oceans is moved by tides and storms and broken by jagged rocks and huge waves. The surfaces of big lakes are shaken by currents and unsettled by winds. Countless creatures live in or close to these deep waters—whales, sea snakes, turtles, eels, and otters. Perhaps all of these things are sometimes mistaken for monsters—or perhaps monsters really live and hide among them.

A small Architeuthis Dux, or giant squid, the origin of the kraken myth. Even one this size could easily sink a fishing boat.

74

THE KRAKEN

Imagine something rising to the surface of the sea like a small island. It measures almost 40 ft. (12m) from end to end. As it appears, it sends waves rolling outward—as it submerges, it drags the water into a whirlpool. It has ten thrashing tentacles, unblinking eyes the size of dinner plates, and the power to fight whales. Clearly, no such creature could ever exist, and yet it does. It is the giant squid and is most likely the source of the fearsome kraken legends. Dramatic stories have been told of one eating a drowning sailor. There is a tale of an especially aggressive squid attacking a Norwegian naval vessel until it got caught in the propellers and was torn to pieces. The stories may be truth or myth, but the animal, though rarely seen, is most definitely real.

Mokele Mbembe eats plants but will knock humans out of their boats and will attack hippos.

MOKELE MBEMBE

In the rain forests of Cameroon, in west Africa, people speak of a dragon in the swamps and lakes around the Congo river basin. It is the size of an elephant, with a leathery hide and a long neck. They call it Mokele Mbembe, "one who stops the flow of rivers." People seem to be describing a dinosaur, perhaps a dwarf *Brontosaurus*. There have been more reports of dinosaurlike creatures from other parts of the world. Some say that they cannot be real because dinosaurs have been extinct for millions of years. But the coelecanth—an ancient and primitive fish that came into being 360 million years ago—was said to be extinct until schools of them were found off the coast of South Africa.

In Lake Okanagan in Canada, Lake Störsjon in Sweden, and Lake Ikeda in Japan, creatures have been glimpsed that look like plesiosaurs. Nessie (above) has been seen in Loch Ness in Scotland since ancient times.

Land monsters

Once, maps bore the words "Here Be Dragons" because no one knew what lay beyond. Now modern transportation reaches farther and farther. Radar, sonar, and infrared cameras explore underground and underwater. Satellites examine the world from above. Yet, still, there are remote, wilderness areas, rarely visited by humans, and the stories of monsters begin there.

Andre Clayton of Springbrook, in Queensland, Australia, with a cast he made from one of nine apparent Yowie tracks in 1998.

MAN APES OR APE-MEN?

Descriptions of these creatures, from all over the world, are remarkably similar. They are all said to walk upright, to be as much as 6.5 ft. (2m) tall, and to be covered with hair. With very few exceptions, they are not aggressive and will run if startled. Yet, in almost 200 years of eyewitness accounts, all we have are a few photographs of distant figures or large footprints. Not a single one has been captured, alive or dead. The Yeti, living in the vast Himalaya mountains in south Asia and respected by Sherpas and holy men, could easily avoid being captured. But in places with many hunters, how have the Canadian Sasquatch and the North American Bigfoot (left) avoided bullets? Also, if the Yowie of Australia is an ape, how did it get there? Humans are the only primates in Australia, and they arrived by boat. However, if these creatures are not real, why do so many people believe in them? Could they be memories awoken by our imaginations? Could memories of life from our ancient ancestors have somehow survived, being inherited by each generation, up to the present day?

CHUPACABRA

If the Yeti and its
relatives turn out to be
creatures of our imaginations,
then the Chupacabra is a beast of
our nightmares. First reported in
Puerto Rico, it seems to have extended
its range throughout Mexico and Central America,
then north into the U.S., and south into Chile and
Brazil. Its name means "goatsucker," and its goat victims
are found with puncture marks, drained of blood. It also
preys on cows, sheep, geese, and ducks and sometimes
bites completely through the skull in order to eat the
brain. In most places the official explanation is that the
dead animals must have been killed by wild dogs or
pumas. It's true that large teams of well-organized
volunteer hunters have failed to corner a Chupacabra—
but then they did not find a pack of dogs or a puma either.
If it does exist, is it a previously unknown animal, a pet
abandoned by an alien spacecraft, or a genetic experiment
that went horribly wrong? No one has the answer—yet.

*Those who have glimpsed the
Chupacabra say that it walks
upright on reptilian legs and
has clawed hands and feet
and vampirelike fangs.*

Alien cats

This alien cat was shot dead in Lellas, Scotland, in 1983.

There is something padding through long grass in the British countryside or crossing a road in the dim light of dusk. It looks big, but it is hard to judge just how big. It might be a dog or a fox, but it moves like a cat. Could it be an ABC—an Alien Big Cat? There have been thousands of sightings, but many people remain unconvinced.

THE POSSIBILITIES

ABCs are large cats that live in Africa, India, or the Americas and are alien to the United Kingdom. The cats might have escaped from zoos or wildlife parks. Or they might have been owned illegally as pets and then released when they grew to full size. Large cats could live wild in the U.K., especially in remote areas, feeding on rabbits, birds, and lambs. Another possibility is the Scottish wildcat, but it is not large enough to be a convincing candidate.

THE CASE AGAINST

Although societies and organizations have been set up that are dedicated to tracking down ABCs, there is not much proof of their existence. Large paw prints and the carcasses of savaged lambs have usually turned out to be the work of dogs. No ABC corpses, skeletons, or even clumps of fur have turned up—except for the "find" of a leopard skull on Bodmin moor in Cornwall, England. The skull was genuine, but it had been taken from an old leopard-skin rug. Almost all photographs of ABCs have been blurry, with nothing in the picture to show the real size of the cat. Also, if every reported sighting was genuine, there would be more big cats in the U.K. than in Africa.

All cats are good at hiding and prefer to hunt at dusk or after dark. This could explain why they are so difficult to track down. ABCs include pumas, lynx (below, left), and black leopards (often called black panthers).

The skull found on Bodmin moor of the so-called Beast of Bodmin is only one of many big cat hoaxes that have fooled the public and even experts.

THE EVIDENCE

Though there have been honest mistakes, a number of reports are significant. Many have come from farmers who are used to looking at animals and are likely to know the difference between a large tomcat, a big black dog, and an ABC. Importantly, a lynx was shot in Suffolk in 1980. In the same year, a puma was caught in Scotland (named Felicity, she was taken to a wildlife park, where she lived for years, and is now stuffed and on display at Inverness Museum). In 2001 a lynx was caught in north London. She is now in Amneville Zoo in France, taking part in a European lynx-breeding program. As these sightings were genuine, could some of the rest be too?

The lonely sight of a small, empty boat,
marooned on a glass-smooth lake,
symbolizes the fate of the disappeared.
Just as there are no oars and no wake,
so there are often no clues or solutions.

CHAPTER SIX

DISAPPEARANCES

It is common knowledge that possessions—books, pens, socks—occasionally vanish. When it happens to people, however, it is much stranger and more unsettling. Some people choose to disappear and start new lives. Others are lost in accidents or wars. Most cases are solved, sometimes after many years. A few remain mysterious forever. Of these, an extraordinarily high number have taken place in a notorious area called the Bermuda Triangle—or have they?

BERMUDA TRIANGLE

This enormous ocean area is defined by imaginary lines joining three points—Bermuda, Miami in Florida, and San Juan in Puerto Rico. Its reputation as a strange and dangerous location is based on the disappearances of ships and aircraft within its invisible boundaries. More than that, there have been reports of strange effects in the sky and sea and of the sudden and unexplained failure of navigational instruments.

The Bermuda Triangle is an area of sudden storms where compasses sometimes give false readings. It is likely that Flight 19 became lost and ran out of fuel.

FLIGHT 19

On December 5, 1945, five TBM Avenger Torpedo Bombers left the U.S. Naval Air Station in Fort Lauderdale, Florida, on a navigation training flight. All had qualified pilots, and a senior flight instructor piloted the lead plane. Two hours into the flight, a radio message between two of the planes was intercepted at the base. It seemed that the in-flight compasses were not working, and the pilots were unsure where they were. Atmospheric static made it impossible for the base to make contact. The flight was never heard from again, and no trace of the aircraft was ever found. Flight 19 is probably the most famous victim of the infamous Bermuda Triangle.

THE MISSING

The list of the missing is long. It includes the *USS Cyclops*, a 19,360-ton coal ship, with a crew of more than 300, which disappeared without a trace in March 1918; the *Marine Sulphur Queen*, with a crew of 39 and a 15,000-ton cargo, in February 1963; the British South American Airways' *Star Tiger*, with six crew members and 25 passengers, in January 1948; her sister plane, *Star Ariel,* in 1949; and a Douglas DC3 in December 1948.

This broken board, found by John Allmand Jr. and his father on a beach in Miami in 1963, is almost certainly from the lost Marine Sulphur Queen.

THEORIES AND BELIEFS

Theories include demonic intervention, kidnapping by alien spacecraft, or a portal opening into another dimension.

A belief strongly held by many is that there have been no more losses in the Bermuda Triangle than in any other tract of water of this size, especially as it carries an enormous amount of both sea and air traffic and is subject to sudden major storms. According to this theory, there is no mystery.

However, there have been survivors who have brought back strange stories. Pilots have reported instrument malfunctions and a curious yellowish sky; sea captains have described an unexpected—and almost fatal—lack of buoyancy in the water.

POSSIBILITIES

Besides dangerous weather conditions or poor navigation, there are two main possibilities.

One: large deposits of methane gas, formed by the rotting of ancient forests, may erupt from the ocean floor. In other areas of the world, drilling ships and rigs have been sunk by this gas, which is highly inflammable and also reduces the sea's buoyancy. This gas is lighter than air, so it would rise into the atmosphere. There, it could cause a passing plane to explode or the engines to fail owing to lack of oxygen.

Two: a survey by the *Seasat* satellite in 1978 showed a huge circular depression in the contour of the ocean within the Triangle. This suggests that a vast meteorite could have landed there in the distant past. If so, its iron mass could cause navigational instruments to give false readings.

Missing at Sea

Disappearances at sea may be unexplained, but they are not necessarily mysterious. Oceans are dangerous places. Sudden storms, bad navigation, or an inexperienced crew can bring a ship to tragedy, and, once sunk into the depths, it might never be found. Someone falling overboard may also vanish. These disappearances may leave questions unanswered, but sometimes something happens that is completely baffling.

Pirate raids were a serious danger to sailing ships, which might be looted and sunk.

MARY CELESTE

A two-masted brigantine called *Amazon* was built in Canada in 1860. The ship had a series of owners and was involved in several minor accidents. There were rumors that she was jinxed. When fixed and sold again, her sname was changed— which is very unlucky, according to superstitions.

On November 7, 1872, now called *Mary Celeste*, the ship sailed from New York City toward Genoa, Italy, with a cargo of 1,700 barrels of alcohol. On December 5, she was sighted, sailing erratically, by the crew of the *Dei Gratia*. She did not respond to signals. A boarding party (right) found no one at the wheel—in fact, no one was on board at all. She was a ghost ship, with her cargo still intact. A lifeboat, the ship's log, and navigational instruments were missing, but no supplies or belongings had been taken. The *Mary Celeste* was towed into Gibraltar, and two official investigations failed to discover what had happened.

The Theories

In 1883 Sir Arthur Conan Doyle, who later created the character Sherlock Holmes, published a story about the ship, which he called *Marie Celeste*, and invented a tale of Barbary pirates who overran it and left it empty and drifting. This opened the door to other theories. Was everyone on board kidnapped by aliens or mermaids, dragged overboard by a giant squid, or frightened into fleeing by a ghostly apparition? Maybe a huge wave washed them overboard. Or, perhaps most likely, rough seas made the captain fear that the inflammable cargo might explode, and he made a disastrous decision to take to the lifeboat, which sank in stormy weather. The stories—and the mystery—may never end.

A Postscript

When the investigations were over, the unfortunate *Mary Celeste* sailed again, under several owners, until her last captain deliberately guided her to her doom on a coral reef in Haiti. Then he and the first mate submitted an insurance claim for a very valuable cargo. But the ship took revenge—she refused to sink completely, wedging herself on the reef, covered only by shallow water. Insurance inspectors were able to examine the "precious" freight. It turned out to be cat food and old rubber boots, and the two men were successfully prosecuted. In 2001 shipwreck hunter Dr. Clive Cussler found her remains, with the coral reef already growing around and over her. Her story is finished— yet still she sails on, through the imaginations of millions who long to discover the truth about her most famous voyage.

Missing on Land

There are extraordinary stories of people walking away from friends or family members and vanishing before their eyes, simply ceasing to exist, as if swallowed up by the air. Each story carries names, places, and dates—but when any of these have been checked, it has turned out that no such person existed in the first place. The stories were local legends, passed on as facts. Some disappearances, though, are well documented.

THE KING'S OWN SANDRINGHAMS

The 5th Territorial Battalion, the Royal Norfolk Regiment, was formed from staff at the royal estate of Sandringham in England. In August 1915, during the World War I Gallipoli campaign in Turkey, the soldiers charged against the Turks. None were seen again. Then, in 1965, four veterans described seeing strange clouds on that day, 50 years earlier. They said that one cloud was low, and the battalion's charge led them into it. The cloud rose and drifted away—and they were gone.

Yet, in 1918, searchers found what remained of 122 men, shot in the head. The Turkish army rarely took prisoners—and a Norfolk Regimental cap badge and shoulder flashes suggested the shocking truth.

The real mystery is that the tale of abduction by alien clouds still persists. Perhaps it seems to be a gentler ending than the cruel reality.

The lost Royal Norfolk Regiment was formed of butlers, laborers, grooms, and gardeners from the royal country retreat at Sandringham.

THE VANISHING LIGHTHOUSE KEEPERS

In December 1900, the *Hesperus* made a routine supply trip to Flannan lighthouse on Eilean Mor, Scotland. Unusually, the flag was not raised in welcome, nor did the three keepers appear to help unload the ship. There was no response to the boat's horn or to a flare. After landing, the crew found the lighthouse deserted. Two oilskin coats were missing, and a chair had been knocked over. The last entry in the log noted a bad storm, but why would all the men go outside in extreme weather, one presumably without a coat?

Rumors grew. It was said that the island was haunted and that a ghost terrified the keepers into the sea; they were seized by a giant sea creature or a foreign vessel; one man went crazy and drowned his companions and then himself.

The loss remains unexplained unless . . . possibly two of the men went out to inspect the storm damage. A freak wave knocked over one, and the other ran to get the third, who knocked over his chair and raced out to help—and a second freak wave completed the tragedy.

A painting by Jeremy Geddes showing the captain of the Hesperus *reading the last entry in the log at the abandoned lighthouse.*

Missing from the Air

Occasionally, something bad happens to an aircraft. Its engines malfunction or it runs out of fuel; instruments fail and the pilot gets lost; it crashes into a mountain or is shot down. If the plane is flying over a remote area at the time, it could be years before it is found and the reason discovered. Sometimes, though, the fate of a plane—or even a single passenger—remains unexplained.

THE LAST FLIGHT OF AMELIA EARHART

In 1937 American aviator Amelia Earhart (1898–1937) was the first person to fly from the Red Sea to India, as part of her attempt to fly around the world. With almost 7,000 mi. (11,000km) of Pacific Ocean ahead, she left Lae, New Guinea, for Howland Island, but she never arrived. A huge, but unsuccessful, search left an unsolved mystery. The U.S. Coast Guard cutter *Itasca*, sailing off Howland Island, picked up a last transmission: "We must be on you but cannot see you . . . gas is running low."

One theory blames the *Itasca*, saying that it should have transmitted a guiding signal for Amelia, and that, lost and out of fuel, she crashed into the ocean. Others believe that she landed on an uninhabited island or that she was diverted by Japanese planes to Saipan island and imprisoned. The last sounds far-fetched—except for the testimony of a young marine who found her briefcase full of maps and documents on Saipan during World War II. He handed it to an officer, but it has since disappeared. No wreckage or remains have ever been located.

THE MYSTERY OF DEVIL'S BRIDGE

In 1999 people in a village near Devil's Bridge in central Wales noticed three military aircraft flying overhead, and then one disappeared and smoke was seen rising up from a thick woodland that was close by. The emergency services were alerted, and a thorough investigation followed— but no wreckage was found, ever. Even more interestingly, the Ministry of Defense was adamant that no aircraft was missing. Mass hallucination seems unlikely— so where did the plane come from and where did it go?

Although Cooper was never found, in 1980 some $20 bills with serial numbers matching the notes given to him turned up on a riverbank on the route of the flight.

THE VANISHING PASSENGER

In 1971 a man calling himself D. B. Cooper hijacked a Northwest Orient 727 airplane flying out of Portland, Oregon. Claiming to have a bomb, he directed the pilot to land in Seattle, Washington, where he swapped some of the crew and all of the passengers for $200,000 in $20 bills and four parachutes. Then he ordered the pilot to fly to Reno, Nevada, with the cabin unpressurized. Before they arrived, a warning light showed that the rear door was open—and Cooper, the money, and the parachutes were gone. Cooper inspired theories, rumors, books, and songs—but his true fate has never been discovered.

These three bridges, one above the other, were given the name Devil's Bridge because it was thought that only the devil could succeed in spanning such a deep and difficult gorge.

The tor (hill) in Glastonbury, England, with the ruined tower of the 14th-century chapel of St. Michael, is a site of tremendous power. Before the draining of the marshes, it was an island and a sacred Celtic site —possibly the magical isle of Avalon itself, where King Arthur is said to be buried.

Chapter seven
Ancient mysteries

The ancient past will always be mysterious. It is like another country but one we can never visit—unless we invent the technique of time travel! All we have are signs and stories, and we cannot always understand these. Stonehenge and the pyramids still puzzle us, despite centuries of research and study. We cannot even be sure if that great British king of long ago, Arthur, was a living man, a powerful legend, or a mixture of the two.

King Arthur and the Holy Grail

Arthur and the Holy Grail are both real and legendary, their stories so complex that the truth is as hard to find as the Grail itself. The Grail, known about for centuries, appeared to Arthur and his knights as if by magic. To each, it gave food and a sense of sacred mystery before disappearing. So began the quest to find it again—and the large collection of stories describing each knight's endeavors.

THE REAL ARTHUR

King Arthur was most likely a Celtic chieftain who rose to power some time during the A.D. 400s or 500s. The Romans had withdrawn from Great Britain, and the country was under attack from all sides, especially by the Saxons. Arthur was a warrior, skilled horseman, and strong leader. He won many victories—and then passed into legend.

This image of King Arthur as a warrior comes from A Chronicle Of England, *published in French verse in the early 1300s.*

THE LEGENDARY ARTHUR

The numerous Arthurian tales were developed and passed on by word of mouth, through bards and storytellers. Geoffrey of Monmouth first wrote them down in 1136 in his imaginative *History of the Kings of Britain*. Of the many versions over the years, most say that Arthur's birth was predicted by the magician Merlin and heralded by a comet. They tell of his court at Camelot, of his fellowship of knights, and of the round table that he had crafted, on Merlin's advice, so that all could be seated equally. They describe his queen, Guinevere, his magical sword, Excalibur, and his death at the hands of Mordred, his son by the enchantress Morgan le Fay.

THE HOLY GRAIL

The Holy Grail is usually thought of as the cup used by Jesus at the Last Supper when he shared wine with his disciples. It is said that Jesus' uncle Joseph of Arimathea used the Grail to catch a few drops of blood at the crucifixion before hiding it in Glastonbury, England. Earlier stories, though, speak of the Grail as a magical cauldron, containing the gift of knowledge, of plenty, or of rebirth after death. Yet others say that the Grail is not an object at all but is spiritual enlightenment. All suggest that only those who are pure in heart will ever find it. Certainly the Grail is powerful, mysterious, and either lost or hidden. There are said to be Grail guardians, who pass on the secret of its location to only a trusted few, and Grail enemies, who would like to use it for evil.

In William Morris' Vision of the Holy Grail, three of Arthur's knights, Galahad, Bors, and Percival, find the sacred cup.

The Grail has been sought for at least 2,000 years, and this is still the case. Many chalices are said to be the true Grail, including this one in the Cathedral of Valencia in Spain.

93

Standing Stones and Spheres

They are found in many parts of the world, alone or in rows or groups, often some distance from the quarries where they were hacked out of the ground. Heavy to shift and hard to shape, their purpose must have been very clear to those who set them in place. Yet now, a few thousand years later, our understanding of them is uncertain and patchy.

CARNAC

There are exceptional prehistoric sites in Great Britain, the Orkney Islands, and Scandinavia, but most impressive of all is the one near Carnac in Brittany, France. There, row upon row of stones stretch for over a mile. Where they cross fields and moors, they are weatherworn and scattered with lichen. Among the trees of the forest of Petit Menéc, they are camouflaged with green moss. Many stones have been taken to repair roads or build walls, but thousands remain—although it is not certain that they are all in their original places. Beyond the lines are stone circles and the remains of tombs. There is no doubt that this was once a hugely important place, but it is so complex that it is not easy to interpret it today.

MYSTERY HILL

On a hillside north of Boston, Massachusetts, there are structures whose age and purpose can only be guessed at. An enormous stone table, known as the Sacrificial Stone, has a groove around the edge, possibly to catch blood. A shaft underneath opens onto an underground chamber, where a priest or shaman could have spoken words that would seem to come out of the earth itself. All around are standing stones, underground structures, tunnels, and strange carvings. Most of the stone was taken to construct buildings in the 1700s, but enough remains to show that it could have been an observatory, predicting the summer and winter solstices. But who made it? Some believe that it has so much in common with Celtic sites in Europe that the Celts must have crossed the Atlantic Ocean centuries before Christopher Columbus (1451–1506) did.

Menhir is Breton for "long stone," and at least one of the Carnac stones is more than 19 ft. (6m) tall.

The stone globes of Costa Rica range from a few inches to 6.5 ft. (2m) in diameter.

THE STONE GLOBES OF COSTA RICA

These spheres of stone are not natural formations; they were made by humans, some time between 200 B.C. and A.D. 800. Originally there may have been hundreds around the Diquis delta of Costa Rica, yet no one seemed to pay much attention to them until the 1930s or 1940s. Since then, they have been examined and studied—but also taken as decorations for buildings and gardens and even blown up by people who thought that they might contain gold. So few are in their original places that it is impossible to know if their positions were important, and no one can explain why they were made or what they were used for.

Stonehenge and Avebury

Stonehenge is probably the most important and best known prehistoric monument. Avebury, also in Wiltshire in southern England, is less famous but possibly more atmospheric. The stones in Avebury, which are spread over a wider area than Stonehenge, have a village built among them—and partly out of them. Both have been studied for centuries, but their purpose is still uncertain.

STONEHENGE

Stonehenge (right) was set in place on the bleak Wiltshire plains around 4,000 years ago. There were at least three separate phases of building, over around 1,000 years. Neolithic long barrows and Bronze Age burial mounds are all around, and burials and cremations have been found among—and even under—the stones themselves. Stonehenge has been called a cemetery, a temple, a setting for ceremonies and festivals, an ancient computer, and an astronomical observatory. Possibly it was all of these. Certainly the heel stone, just outside the circle, is placed so that the midsummer sun rises directly over it. Other parts are aligned with sunset at the winter solstice and with midsummer moonrise.

AVEBURY

In Avebury there is a stone circle with a rampart, a ditch, and avenues of stones, built around 2500 to 2000 B.C. The meaning is difficult to decipher because it has been badly damaged. In the Middle Ages, the circle was thought to be the devil's work, and many of the stones were laid across fire pits and smashed. In the 1500s and 1600s, some were removed in order to build a village within the site.

From the 1700s, Avebury was taken seriously as an ancient monument, but the site was plagued by amateur archaeologists. They dug pits and shifted stones and caused so much disorder and damage that it is now impossible to say exactly how the structure was originally laid out.

THE BUILDING OF STONEHENGE

One thing is certain—in its time, Stonehenge was extremely important. The effort needed to build it would have been immense. The stone used in the large uprights is local, though each still had to be moved, shaped, levered into predug pits, and placed upright, and then the lintel stones were raised into place. The bluestones of the inner ring were even more labor-intensive because they come from the Prescelly mountains in Wales. At one time no one believed that humans could have moved them such a great distance and thought that the wizard Merlin (right) must have carried them by magic.

Wonders of the South

When the Spanish conquered South America in the 1500s, they killed many of the inhabitants and destroyed almost everything that they had built or woven or crafted from metal and precious stones. They wrote of delicate ornaments, including a gold fountain with golden threads for water that were then melted down. They wrecked monumental structures. Yet what remains is still magnificent.

A gold decoration of Inti, the Inca sun god. The Incas called gold "the sweat of the sun" and silver "the tears of the moon."

LOST CITY IN THE CLOUDS

The Incan ruins lie between the high granite peaks of Huayna Picchu and Machu Picchu, not far from the ancient capital, Cuzco, in Peru. It is a dramatic landscape, reaching up into the clouds and plunging down into deep gorges where the Urubamba river races toward the sea.

The Spanish did not discover the Machu Picchu area when they wiped out the vast and powerful Inca Empire in the 1500s. It was not until 1911 that an outsider, Hiram Bingham (1875–1956), found it and reported back. Today the terraces, ruined dwellings, temples, food storehouses, and ceremonial plaza are visited by thousands of tourists. Even so, the magic and mystery of the place remain unspoiled.

Sacsayhuaman was built with enormous blocks of stone, dragged from a quarry almost 2 mi. (3km) away.

SACSAYHUAMAN

North of the ancient Inca capital, Cuzco, whose name means "navel of the world," lie the foundations of a vast fortress. The puma was the symbol of the Inca emperors, and Cuzco is said to be puma-shaped, with Sacsayhuaman as its head. All that remains of this most impressive of monuments are its ramparts (walls). The stones are carved with such skill that they fit together perfectly, with no gaps and no need for mortar to hold them in place. No one now can say why—or even how—it was built, but it is so awe-inspiring that the Spanish conquistadores could not believe that human hands had constructed it. They decided that it must have been the work of evil spirits.

In the Pacific Ocean, halfway between Chile and Tahiti, lies tiny Easter Island (Rapa Nui). There stand huge, mysterious rock figures, known as moai, carved centuries ago, probably by the ancestors of the present-day inhabitants. Some keep silent watch out to sea, and some keep vigil inland. No one knows for sure how or why the statues were erected.

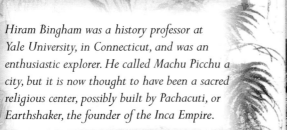

Hiram Bingham was a history professor at Yale University, in Connecticut, and was an enthusiastic explorer. He called Machu Picchu a city, but it is now thought to have been a sacred religious center, possibly built by Pachacuti, or Earthshaker, the founder of the Inca Empire.

99

ANCIENT EGYPTIAN CREATIONS

*S*ecrets and mysteries remain, but much of what is known about ancient Egypt was revealed by a single discovery. A stone found near the town of Rosetta in A.D. 1799 was carved with the same announcement in Greek, in hieroglyphics, and in demotic (simplified hieroglyphs). This was the key to translating the inscriptions on monuments and within the pyramids.

The Great Sphinx's outstretched forelegs measure almost 50 ft. (15m). The figure is very weatherworn and is often partially covered by drifting sand.

THE SPHINX

The Great Sphinx on the Plateau of Giza is carved from an outcrop of limestone bedrock. It has the body of a resting lion and the head of a pharaoh and is more than 147 ft. (45m) long. It lies as if guarding the Pyramid of Khafre. Between its paws stands the Dream Stela—a stone slab with an inscription. According to this, more than 3,000 years ago Prince Thutmose fell asleep in its shade. In a dream, the Sphinx promised that if the prince freed it from the sand, he would become king. He did—and became Thutmose IV (b. 1425 B.C.).

One of Khufu's funeral boats (below), discovered at his pyramid. It was found dismantled in a boat pit in 1954—it took ten years to reassemble it. Before the discovery of the boat, three empty pits, such as the one above, were uncovered. But why were they empty?

THE GREAT PYRAMID OF CHEOPS

The Great Pyramid was built for Pharaoh Khufu, often called by his Greek name, Cheops. Inside, it is complex and is different from any other pyramid. It has three chambers, the third containing the royal sarcophagus (coffin). This was empty when it was first officially opened. In 2004 two French Egyptologists, using a radar scanner, found a corridor deep inside. They thought that this could lead to a fourth room at the center of the pyramid, but it has not yet been explored.

Inserting the robot into one of the shafts in the Great Pyramid.

UNEXPLAINED SHAFTS

Unlike the other pyramids, the Great Pyramid has four narrow shafts. The two upper ones lead outward from the king's chamber, emerging high up on the north and south sides of the pyramid. The two lower ones lead outward from close to the queen's chamber, though they do not enter it, nor do they emerge through the outside walls. All four are too narrow for a human to pass through and would have been extremely difficult to construct, so they must be of great importance. It has been suggested that the two from the king's chamber were intended to link his spirit with stars in the sky. Yet, why two, pointing in different directions? And why, when Rudolf Gantenbrink sent a small robot with a camera along one of the lower shafts, did it reveal a polished stone "door" with two copper fittings? Again, further exploration has yet to be undertaken.

Map of El Dorado by Sir Walter Raleigh (1552–1618), an English courtier, adventurer, and soldier. In 1595 he led an expedition to South America to find the fabled land. Like all the others, it failed.

CHAPTER EIGHT

LOST LANDS AND SECRETS

For centuries, quests and expeditions have been undertaken to reveal ancient cities deep in the rain forests; elaborate graves of pharoahs beneath Egyptian sands; forgotten temples; and tunnels and tombs. Many have been found. Some, such as Atlantis and El Dorado, remain elusive. The most important lost land of all, though—and the one with the richest treasures—can be rediscovered by anyone who tries. It is the land of the imagination.

Atlantis

The island of Lemuria is now thought to be the Seychelles in the Indian Ocean.

F or hundreds of years, people have dreamed of lands lost under the sea. *Arthurian legends tell of Lyonesse, off the U.K. Isles of Scilly. An obscure book,* Oera Linda, *records a place called Atland, off the Netherlands. James Churchward (1852–1936) wrote of Mu, or Lemuria, suggesting that its peaks formed the Polynesian islands. But the most famous of them all is Atlantis.*

THE BEGINNINGS

The first writings about Atlantis (below) came from Greek philosopher Plato (427–347 B.C.). According to him, the tale originated in ancient Egypt and was passed on by word of mouth for 900 years before he told it in two texts, *Timaeus* and *Critias*. Plato described a lush, rich land and an advanced society. He said that the entire civilization was lost in a day, in a cataclysm of earthquakes and floods, as punishment by the gods for becoming materialistic and corrupt. Its sunken mass lay deep under the Atlantic Ocean, beyond Gibraltar.

LAND OF THE GOLDEN AGE

Many who believe in Atlantis describe it as a land from a lost golden age. They say that it is where all culture began. It was sophisticated and technologically advanced, and when it flourished in the middle of the Atlantic, its people took their knowledge and skills to the lands around the ocean—South America, North Africa, and Europe. Some people regard its existence as the only explanation for the fact that all of these countries have a version of the story of Atlantis and that there are similarities between their cultures. On the other hand, scientist Thor Heyerdahl (1914–2002) and others have demonstrated that long-distance ocean travel in primitive boats was possible in the distant past, so a linking landmass was not essential.

Did Plato write an historical truth or create a fable about Atlantis in order to make a philosophical point? Some believe that he was referring to the destruction of the volcanic island of Thera, near Crete, around 1500 B.C. This may have been responsible for the end of the Minoan civilization, which was not unlike Plato's description of the Atlanteans.

THE SEARCH FOR ATLANTIS

There are numerous books and articles, explorations, and theories devoted to Atlantis. Several psychics and mediums say that they have visited it while in a trance—though it is unclear whether this means that it is a physical place or a state of mind. Explorers have made discoveries on the ocean floor. Could the North Atlantic Ridge be part of the sunken land? Are the Portuguese Azores the tips of Atlantis' sunken mountains? Is the island of Spartel, northwest of Africa, a likely remnant?

Shangri-la and El Dorado

When you are searching for a mysterious place or a lost city, it is useful to know what you are looking for. Otherwise, you may not know when you have found it. It is also helpful if it is real. The well-known vision of Shangri-la was, and still is, real—though not physically so. El Dorado was almost certainly physically real, but it was not what its seekers believed it to be.

SHANGRI-LA

The name of Shangri-la, the lost kingdom behind the Himalaya mountains, was created in the 1930s by James Hilton in his novel *Lost Horizon*. This was an idyllic place, overseen by wise Tibetan monks, where wisdom and peace prevailed. The book was filmed twice, and Shangri-la has come to symbolize an earthly paradise.

The fictional Shangri-la was almost certainly based on the legendary land of Shambhala, also said to be hidden behind the Himalayas in an area of mountains and lakes sacred to Hindus and Buddhists. Many, though, believe that Shambhala is actually a state of mind—a sense of peace and joy achieved by meditation.

Hundreds of people have sought to find the geographical location of Shambhala, searching the remote mountains on the borders of India and China or in the isolated valleys below.

106

EL DORADO

Dorado is Spanish for "golden" or "gilded," so El Dorado means "the golden one." When the Spanish arrived in South America early in the 1500s, they found an abundance of gold. Still, they wanted more, and when they heard talk of "the golden one," they imagined a great city made from the precious metal.

THE GOLDEN ONE

Like Shangri-la, El Dorado is now part of our language, either meaning a place of spiritual beauty or a place of unimaginable riches. One of the first of the numerous expeditions to find the city of gold was led by Gonzalo Jiménez de Quesada, the founder of Bogotá, Colombia, in 1539. He succeeded in discovering El Dorado— but he did not recognize it. Watching the coronation ceremony of the Chibcha Indians, he saw the new king ceremonially covered with clay and then sprinkled with powdered gold, until he became completely golden. He sat on a raft on Lake Guatavita, with gifts for the god of the lake, and then dived in himself until the gold was washed away into the water. When he returned to the shore, he was confirmed as the king.

It is unlikely that there ever was a city of gold. El Dorado, the golden one, was really a glittering gilded man.

THE HOLLOW EARTH

There is an ancient and mysterious region beneath the surface of Earth. Mythologies call it the underworld, the shadowy spirit land of the dead. Explorers see it as a place of cave systems, potholes, tunnels, and subterranean lakes—some mapped, many unknown. But none of this goes all the way to the core of the planet—unless it has a stranger interior structure than can easily be imagined.

SPHERES WITHIN SPHERES

No one has ever explored the center of our planet, so how can anyone know what is in there? Today the answer can be computed, probably accurately, but not everyone is convinced that it is as simple as that.

Edmund Halley (1656–1742), a brilliant scientist and astronomer, successfully calculated the cycle of our brightest comet, which was then named after him. He also studied Earth's magnetic field and noticed that its direction varies slightly. To account for this, he put forward a theory that Earth is made of four spheres (right), one inside the other like Russian dolls, each with its own magnetic field. He thought that there may be a gaseous atmosphere within and that escaping gas could account for the natural light shows known as auroras.

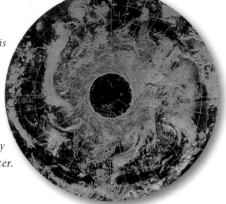

This hole over the North Pole, seen in this photograph taken in 1968, is an illusion. The picture actually shows several images together, taken over 24 hours. All of the pictures were taken in daylight, and the black hole at the top is the portion of the Arctic Circle that is not lit during the day throughout winter.

SECRET ENTRANCES

Some people say that there are two large entrances to Earth, one at each pole. They account for the fact that no aircraft crew, flying over the poles, has seen such an entrance by explaining that planes actually travel around the rims of the holes. Onboard compasses, affected by the magnetic field within the planet, incorrectly show a course right over the center.

Other openings in Earth have been mentioned: behind the high Himalaya mountains in Asia; in Yorkshire, England; in the Matto Grosso region of Brazil; and in Australia, Egypt, and Africa. All are linked by an extensive system of underground tunnels, which is as secret as the entrances themselves.

A WORLD WITHIN THE WORLD

What is inside Earth? It depends on who you listen to. There may be a sun—or even two suns—at its heart and a complex ecosystem of lush vegetation and animals. Perhaps Shambhala (see page 106) is in there or the subterranean kingdom of Agharti. Both of these are said to be communities of spiritually enlightened people, who keep great secrets and wisdom safe until those on the surface understand the futility of war and violence. Atlantis (see pages 104–105)—or a place of refuge for those who would otherwise have died when Atlantis sank—may be inside. Or, as some insist, it could be an entire inner universe from which alien spacecraft emerge to patrol the planet!

The Hunt for Treasures

The fact that something is lost or hidden inspires an urge to search for it. An antique map with the site of buried riches marked on it or a rumor of an ancient ship, sunk with its cargo of gold, have been reasons enough to launch expeditions. The purpose of the hunt is to find the prize, but the quest itself may be the most exciting part.

Tiny flakes of gold may be washed out of rocks by rivers and streams. If the water is scooped up in a pan, the gold sinks to the bottom. Panning for gold is popular in Australia and the Americas.

MONTEZUMA'S TREASURE

Montezuma (1466–1520) was the last Aztec emperor in what is now Mexico. When the Spanish arrived, it seems that the Aztec priests believed that Spanish conquistador Hernán Cortés was their god Quetzalcoatl and offered him lavish gifts. This whetted the Spanish appetite for treasures. They imprisoned Montezuma, planning to rule the Aztecs through him, but the people rebelled and stoned their emperor to death. The Spaniards left but returned to destroy the great Aztec city of Tenochtitlán.

Legends say that before the conquistadores returned, the Aztecs hid some of their treasures. But where? Some say deep in the Guatemalan rain forest. Others favor Utah, where there are caves in Johnson Canyon, created by those who dug for the Aztec gold. In the 1990s, divers exploring a tunnel under a nearby lake met strong currents and weird apparitions and gave up. Was the gold ever there? And, if so, is it still?

THE MONEY PIT

Oak Island, off Nova Scotia in Canada, keeps its secret, even though the oak trees have all died. The hunt began in 1795, when 16-year-old Daniel McGinnis paddled his canoe to the small island to explore. He found a depression in the ground, with a rope and pulley hanging from a branch. This suggested that someone had dug a pit in order to bury something, beginning a treasure hunt that continues today.

Daniel returned with some friends, and they dug down almost 30 ft. (9m), discovering layers of flagstones and then of oak logs, at intervals. Later expeditions reached around 90 ft. (27m) and found a stone tablet with coded writing that allegedly said, "40 feet (12m) below two million pounds are buried." The tablet is long lost, and there are no photographs. The pit flooded, and another was dug beside it, which also flooded. Possibly flood tunnels had been created as booby traps, but perhaps they are natural.

Does the pit contain pirate treasures, the horde of some eccentric person, or nothing but hopes and dreams?

As the years passed, the attempts to find the Money Pit treasure became more sophisticated, expensive, and dangerous (with several accidental deaths)—but no more successful.

There is a belief that if rain is on the way, cows lie down in order to keep some ground dry to stand on later. This is not always true. Sometimes the cow is just resting.

CHAPTER NINE

CURES, SIGNS, AND SKILLS

One mystery is why so much of humanity has forgotten how to work with natural forces and cures. In order to work with them, it is necessary to be aware of them and to understand them. Knowledge comes from study, observation, and experiments, but some people—especially healers and dowsers—seem to have inborn abilities. The color of the dawn sky, the behavior of animals, and the electromagnetic forces in the world are all useful signs to the wise.

Weird or Wonderful?

The natural world is full of cures. The knowledge of these once belonged only to healers, shamans, and wise women. Later scientists began to analyze medicinal plants. They discovered that the healers were right about many of them—including the bark of the willow tree, which can be used to make aspirin, and the herb sage, which can improve memory. But some of the ancient cures were very strange.

One ancient remedy for warts was to touch them with a toad in the hope that they would disappear to join the toad's warts.

OF DOGS AND WARTS

Strange remedies from the past often relied on sympathetic magic. This seeks to cure like with like—or to treat a problem with what causes it. Sometimes it works. However, touching a toad will not take away a wart, and hair from a rabid dog will not heal the victim of its bite.

Rabies, a horrible and often fatal disease, is carried in the saliva of animals that are suffering from it. In medieval Europe, a popular, though ineffective, treatment was to kill a rabid dog and bind a tuft of its hair over the wound.

Ancient folk remedies for warts run into the thousands. They include rubbing the wart with a piece of meat and then burying the meat; rubbing it with an old bone, before throwing the bone over the shoulder; and wrapping it in a fava bean pod. Many of these seemed to work because warts often go away by themselves.

Pressing a cool dock leaf (left) onto the rash caused by a stinging nettle (far left) takes the pain away very quickly (though no one knows for sure why). Luckily, dock and nettles always grow close to each other.

ANIMAL MEDICINE

Wonderful natural remedies are countless and are used by animals as well as people. A few years ago researchers working in Africa noticed chimpanzees eating from two different plants, even though they obviously disliked them. One plant, *vernonia*, is known as bitter leaf. The other, *aspilia*, a creeping sunflower, is also very bitter. Later analysis showed that *vernonia* is good for digestion, and *aspilia* contains a natural antibiotic. Further checking showed that both of these plants have been used in Tanzanian folk medicines for centuries. How wonderful that chimpanzees know where to find plants to cure their ills and eat them even though they taste horrible!

Chimpanzees in Africa have been monitored looking for medicinal plants. Sometimes a chimp seemed very sick, yet it would travel some distance to find the right plant—then made a disgusted face as it chewed on it.

ONE PAIN FOR ANOTHER

This bee remedy is both weird and wonderful. A bee sting hurts because the bee has injected venom into the skin. Surprisingly, that same venom helps reduce the inflammation of a painful condition known as arthritis. Now that this is understood by modern medicine, a doctor can use a syringe to put the venom where it is needed—it is no longer necessary to disturb an entire hive.

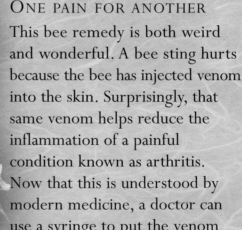

This Peruvian beekeeper's bees rarely sting him.

115

ITCHY FEET AND WEATHER LORE

Before scientific forecasting, people relied on observation to predict the weather, and some old methods are at least as reliable as modern ones. For example, animals and birds really do lie low before severe storms. A halo around the Moon often does promise rain, because the high-altitude moisture causing it usually sinks lower and forms rain-bearing clouds. The significance of itchy feet, however, is almost impossible to prove.

The best-known groundhog is Punxsutawney Phil of Pennsylvania, made even more famous by the movie Groundhog Day *(1993).*

THE SHADOW OF THE GROUNDHOG

The word "woodchuck" comes from *wojak*, the Native American name for the groundhog. It is a type of rodent that lives in North America and hibernates during the winter. Traditionally, it looks out of its burrow on February 2 each year. If it sees its shadow, it goes back to sleep for six weeks, knowing that seeing sunshine so early in the year means a long winter ahead. If it doesn't see a shadow, it stays out, knowing that it can expect a mild spring. (In parts of north Europe, the badger serves the same purpose.) Although Groundhog Day is very famous, records show that the animal is not especially accurate in its predictions.

HANDS, FEET, AND EARS

It is said that if your feet itch for no good reason, you are about to travel and walk on strange ground. If your ears burn, it means that someone is talking about you. The right ear is affected when something nice is being said, the left when it is something nasty. An itchy left hand warns that you will soon have to pay out money; an itchy right hand means that you are about to receive some.

With all of these signs, people generally remember when they are right and not when they are wrong, and it is hard to verify. When your ears burn, how can you find out whether something nice or nasty is being said when you do not know who is talking about you?

BIRDS, BEES, AND ANTS

Birds are often useful weather indicators. Seabirds sense shifts in barometric pressure, which signal weather changes, and move inland when storms are coming. Swallows throughout Europe and Africa fly high when it is dry and low when it is wet and windy. This is because they are following their insect food, which rises on warm thermals (air currents) on dry, sunny days. In Australia, a kookaburra's call is a fairly accurate sign that rain is on the way.

In Europe, Australia, the Americas, and Africa, observe the bees. They return to their hives before bad weather strikes. In China, ants and snakes are the ones to watch. They emerge from underground as rain approaches, for fear of drowning inside their waterlogged burrows.

Hang a piece of seaweed outside to check for rain. If the seaweed becomes dry and crumbly, the air is dry. If the seaweed becomes damp and slimy again, there is moisture around, suggesting that it will rain soon.

RED SKY AT NIGHT

Weather systems usually move west to east in both hemispheres. A red sky in the morning, with the Sun low in the east, is caused by moisture droplets scattering the red wavelength of light sideways. Therefore, rain is likely. In the evening, with the Sun low in the west, a red sky is caused by dust particles. Therefore, the approaching weather system is crossing dry ground, bringing good weather. So, "Red sky at night, shepherd's (or sailor's) delight; red sky in the morning, shepherd's warning" is often true.

SKILLS AND INSTINCTS

How can a sea turtle swim for thousands of miles, yet find her way back to the beach where she was born in order to lay her eggs? How do birds know when and where to migrate? Are they guided by instincts? How can a dowser find underground water with a forked hazel twig or buried metal with a tiny pendulum? Is this instinct or skill—or a mixture of both?

This man is using a metal dowsing rod to search for water. It seems that some people may have an instinctive ability to pick up the tiny electrical signals given off by water, metal, and other materials. Perhaps dowsing is an inborn instinct but one that can be developed into a very real skill.

DOWSING

The first and most important use of dowsing was to find underground water sources in apparently dry areas. This is why it is sometimes called water witching. Dowsers may use forked sticks, which dip when a discovery is made, a pair of rods, which cross each other, or even a small pendulum.

Dowsing's earliest known practitioners were the ancient Egyptians and ancient Chinese—and dowsing is still used today. No one yet knows how it works; yet those with the skill frequently find what they are looking for, including metal, oil, and other buried items.

MIGRATION

Birds, turtles, toads, butterflies, and reindeer are among the many species that migrate—traveling to different areas or even different countries. They may be in search of warmer weather, a better food supply, or the place where they were born in order to lay their own eggs or give birth to their young. Often they cover vast distances, but they rarely, if ever, get lost. What is their secret? Do they navigate by the wind, by the stars, by scent, by sound, or by some form of memory inherited from their ancestors? For hundreds of years, this was an almost magical mystery.

Then, in the 1950s, a study at Frankfurt zoo in Germany showed that some birds that, when free, migrated southwest in the early winter would cluster in the southwest corners of their cages at the appropriate time. The conclusion was that they were responding to Earth's magnetic field, and further research showed that numerous creatures have the same ability.

EARTH'S MAGNETIC FIELD

The movement of molten iron in the center of Earth sends electrical currents outward and upward, creating Earth's magnetic field (below). The field is extremely important, not least because it protects us from cosmic rays, yet we still do not fully understand it.

All living creatures, including these migrating reindeer in Norway, have tiny traces of magnetite inside their brains. Magnetite reacts to Earth's magnetic force field almost like a built-in compass. Our brains also contain magnetite, yet we do not seem to use it. Is this something that we could learn?

119

CHAPTER TEN

LINES AND LABYRINTHS

The spiral is a very ancient symbol. It occurs in nature and is found in the earliest cave paintings and Stone Age rock carvings all over the globe. A labyrinth is formed of a complex spiral that turns back upon itself, perhaps many times. Straight lines are rare in the natural world but have been used by people for thousands of years in order to impose order or meaning on the landscape.

The basic spiral is found throughout nature, from the shape of an ammonite to the structure of a galaxy.

Lines in the Landscape

Lines in the landscape may be natural, formed by rivers or fissures on Earth's surface. They may be invisible, like the paths of Earth's energy, understood by masters of feng shui and other experts. They may be deliberately created, either shaped into patterns or laid out as straight tracks. They may be symbolic routes to be followed by those undertaking a quest. Or they may remain mysterious and unexplained.

Nazca Lines

The Nazca peoples lived in southern Peru, before the Incas, between A.D. 200–600. The lines that bear their name spread over an area of 37 mi. (60km) by 15 mi. (24km) of desert. Many are straight, but some show vast figures of lizards, men, dogs, birds, and spiders. They were first noticed by the outside world in the 1920s, from airplanes. Because they are best seen from above, some people have suggested that they were made by visitors from other planets. But the designs are similar to those on Nazca pottery, and it is more than likely that generation after generation undertook the immense labor of shifting soil and stones to create the outlines in the pale undersoil. The meaning of the Nazca art may be lost, but it is clear that it was once of enormous significance, and great efforts are underway to protect it from mud slides and damage by tourism.

The giant outline of a monkey, crossed by straight lines. At one time, these may have been ritually walked over—to keep the energy flowing or to summon rain.

SONG LINES

The Australian aboriginal Dreamtime (or
Dreaming) is a subtle and complex creation
myth. It is so deeply a part of aboriginal
culture that it is doubtful if any outsider
truly understands it. The songs and stories
speak of the Ancient Ancestors, the first to be
woken from the earth, who moved across the
land, singing the rock, plants, animals, and
people into being. Though the Dreamtime has
passed, the descendants of the Ancestors still
honor them and all they created with songs
and ceremonies. Believing that the sacred is
within everything, they have a deep respect
for the landscape and all that is part of it or
that grows or lives upon it. The Song Lines
lie like an unseen spiritual pattern, left
behind as the Ancestors sang their way
through the landscape.

*Dreamtime figures painted
on Nourlangie rocks in
Arnhem Land, Australia.*

LEY LINES

They were first named ley lines in 1921 by Alfred Watkins, a merchant
and amateur archaeologist. He noticed numerous straight tracks
across the English countryside, with each alignment touching
on several prehistoric sites. These sites included standing
stones and stone circles, megalithic tombs, beacon hills,
and churches built on ancient sacred ground. Many pass
through places with "ley" in their names. Watkins assumed
that they were primitive trading routes. Others interpret them
differently, suggesting that they mark the currents of Earth's energy,
called chi by the feng shui masters.

Mazes and Labyrinths

Both words have the same meaning—a complex formation of twisting paths. "Labyrinth" comes from a word used in Greek mythology for the prison home of a half-man, half-bull creature—the Minotaur (left). It is more often used for religious or symbolic structures. "Maze" is a Middle English word, from the same root as "amazed." It is more often used for structures designed to entertain—such as the maze at Hampton Court Palace in England.

AMAZING MAZES

The first mazes built for entertainment appeared in the 1500s. They were in the grounds of royal palaces in France and England. The most famous in the late 1600s was in Versailles, Paris, but it no longer exists. The most famous today is at Hampton Court Palace in London, England (below), and it is still there. This type of maze, with high hedges, is a practical joke, deliberately planned with dead ends and an indirect route to the center. Just outside stands a tall chair that gives a clear view so that anyone who is lost inside can be "talked" to freedom.

The elaborate labyrinth on the floor of the cathedral in Chartres, near Paris, France. See if you can find your way to the center and back.

SIMPLE LABYRINTHS

The origins of the labyrinth are unknown. Christian tradition says that it was invented by King Solomon. The Indian epic the *Mahabharata* attributes it to Drona, the magician. Yet labyrinths are older than either.

The earliest were simple, just a single twisting path, with only one possible route to the center. They are found in many parts of the world, including India and Indonesia, North Africa and the Americas, and Europe. They may be square or circular. They are not usually three-dimensional—like hedge mazes—but are patterns made on a surface.

These labyrinths were not intended to confuse but rather to draw a person in to the still, quiet center and then allow a slow and gentle return to the outside world.

SACRED LABYRINTHS

These are often more complicated and can be very varied. They are puzzles that must be solved. Some say that they are designed to lure in the devil and leave him lost and bewildered. More often they are believed to suggest the difficulties of the journey through life toward death or enlightenment. They may also stand for the unconscious mind, and the journey to the center may be a journey in search of the self. In many cultures they were used for processions, rituals, or games.

Mazes set in the floors of Christian churches or cathedrals could be followed on foot as a symbolic pilgrimage to the Holy Land. Early Christian worshippers worked their way around them on their knees in order to seek forgiveness for their sins.

CROP CIRCLES

They are called crop or corn circles, but they are not always circular. They may be stars or spirals or other elaborate geometric shapes. They are best seen from a high vantage point, though they are also visible from the ground. They have been reported in Australia, Canada, the Czech Republic, Germany, the Netherlands, and the United States, but most are found in the U.K., especially in Wiltshire and the surrounding counties.

In the 1600s, crop circles were called the work of the devil. A pamphlet published in England in 1678 included this woodcut of the Mowing Devil at work.

EARLY CIRCLES

Simple crop circles have probably been around for as long as crops have. They are formed by the bending or flattening of the stems of wheat, barley, or other crops. The stems are usually undamaged and may straighten again after a few days. Many people blamed animals walking at night, heavy flocks of rooks (crows) feeding on the grains, or possibly mini whirlwinds, which are not uncommon in the summer.

In the late 1970s, complicated designs appeared, and by the early 1980s, newspapers and television began to take an interest. From then, the circles grew even more ambitious.

CIRCLES EVERYWHERE

Crop circles are not just patterns in fields (such as the one on the right). In the Czech Republic, trees have been seen bending toward a central point, which may mark an underground spring. In Scandinavia, ice circles form on rivers, possibly caused by currents. Circles in the snow have appeared throughout northern Europe and Canada, while the sand circles of Namibia are a tourist attraction.

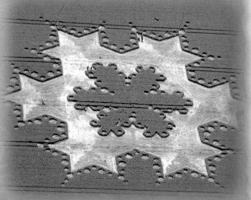

SUPERNATURAL OR NATURAL?

Some crop-circle patterns are ancient Mayan in origin; some show the solar system; others may carry symbolic messages. Could the messages come from the earth itself? Are some the work of extraterrestrials that are attempting contact?

Almost all crop circles appear overnight. People have reported hearing whistling electronic sounds and seeing floating balls of light. One or two who claim to have witnessed a formation say that it hissed as it fanned into shape. In one case, a witness saw a tube of light descend and carve the design.

Possibly they are made by a vortex—a funnel of air like a tornado, but electrically charged. Or maybe they are caused by vibrations. All matter, including Earth itself, is made of vibrating particles. A Swiss scientist, Dr. Hans Jenny, studied the effects of vibrations and showed that different sound frequencies can cause different patterns. But could changes in Earth's vibrations create such detailed circles on its surface?

It is accepted that some elaborate circles are made by landscape artists who are working in secret. But what about the others? Who or what made them? And how and why were they done?

Examinations of some circles have found strange things. Sometimes the crop stems show signs of having been hit by a blast of microwave radiation. More compounds containing magnetic iron have been recovered from inside the circles than from outside. Cameras, cell phones, and other electronic equipment are said to fail if placed within them.

The term "flying saucer" was first used in 1947 by Kenneth Arnold, a pilot who saw several disk-shaped metallic objects in the sky above Washington.

CHAPTER ELEVEN

FROM ANOTHER PLANET

How many stars are in the universe? Once, astronomers said twice as many as there are grains of sand in the world. Now they speak of ten times that number, possibly more. Many are likely to have planets circling them, as Earth and its companions circle the Sun. And some must support life—even scientists who are skeptical about UFOs agree about that. But do alien life-forms visit us, and will we ever be able to visit them?

UFOs and Foo Fighters

The term "UFO" has come to mean "alien spacecraft." In fact, it stands for unidentified flying object and can apply to all types of things that look strange at first but are later identified as something ordinary. Many so-called UFOs turn out to be clouds, weather balloons, hot-air balloons, airships, meteors, aircraft seen from odd angles, or even kites. But what about the ones that are never identified?

FOO FIGHTERS

Globes of colored light were regularly reported by fighter pilots on both sides during World War II. The British first assumed that they were German weapons. The Germans called them Feuerballs, or fireballs. The Americans, inspired by Smokey Joe, a U.S. cartoon character whose catchphrase was "Where there's foo, there's fire," called them Foo Fighters. "Foo Fighters" was the name that stuck.

No one has ever been able to explain them. If they were enemy weapons, why did they never fire on or damage any aircraft? If they were optical illusions, why did pilots and navigators not recognize them as such? If they were ball lightning (see page 62), why would they appear when there was not an electrical storm?

Foo Fighters often flew in formation and were able to maneuver with great skill and speed.

On December 29, 1953, this UFO was photographed in the sky over Bulawayo, Southern Rhodesia (now Zimbabwe).

UFOs

Whether or not some UFOs come from other planets, there are certainly things flying above Earth that have never been explained. People who are familiar with the sky and its air traffic have seen extraordinary sights. The astronomer who discovered the planet Pluto, Clyde W. Tombaugh, observed a group of lights traveling through the New Mexico sky in 1949. Despite his thousands of hours of sky watching, they completely perplexed him.

Is it possible that some UFOs are craft containing time travelers from our own future? Or could it be that they are not solid but are made of lights created by natural energies—earthlights—that are as physically real as the auroras and the planet's magnetic field? Whatever the truth, until they are identified, UFOs will continue to fascinate us.

Lenticular clouds

This skier is on Mauna Kea in Hawaii, watching a lenticular—or lens-shaped—cloud. Clouds like this appear on the lee, or downwind, side of a hill or mountain when strong winds crossing the high ground cause wave motions in the atmosphere. As rising droplets of moisture gather into clouds, the wave effect whisks them into these curious shapes, which can stay in one place for a long time. It is not surprising that they are sometimes mistaken for flying saucers.

Roswell and the Men in Black

The possibility of life visiting from other planets is exciting, but uncertain. Since the 1940s, thousands of people have insisted that they have seen alien spacecraft—and even extraterrestrials—but there has never been undeniable proof. Maybe governments cover up evidence. Maybe witnesses are mistaken. Either way, enthusiasts continue to study past events. The most famous, the Roswell Incident, is around 50 years old.

THE ROSWELL CRASH

In the summer of 1947, something fell from the sky and crashed in Roswell, New Mexico. The headline in the *Roswell Daily Record* on July 8 read: "RAAF captures flying saucers on ranch in Roswell region." Though the news came from a press release issued by the Roswell Army Air Force (RAAF), they denied it almost immediately, saying that the object was a saucer-shaped reflector dish from a weather balloon. Even today, it is not known why they changed their story or what it really was that they found—a weather balloon, a top-secret aircraft or rocket, or, just possibly, an alien spacecraft.

The rancher who found and reported pieces of metal scattered in the desert near Roswell was convinced that it did not come from anything human-made. Senior RAAF officers also said that they were mystified by the strange wreckage.

It is said a nurse at the RAAF base described an alien that looked like this. The nurse has never been traced.

CAPTURED ALIENS

Those who believe that an alien craft—
or possibly two—crashed in Roswell are
also convinced that it contained an alien crew.
Witnesses came forward, at the time and later
on, to say that they had seen the bodies of
dead aliens that were taken into the base for
forensic examination. Others insist that aliens
have been captured alive, at Roswell and other
crash sites, and taken to the so-called Area 51,
a U.S. Air Force site in the Nevada desert.
There, it is said, lies a massive underground
"city" where aliens and humans work together
on covert projects. Could such a big secret
have been kept for such a long time by so
many people? We may never know.

THE MEN IN BLACK

Are the Men in Black government agents
or aliens? Or do they only exist in the
imaginations of those who claim to have met
them? There are numerous reports of Men
in Black visiting people who believe that they
have seen an alien spacecraft or found debris
fallen from one. There are usually three men,
all identical, with black suits and hats,
blank faces, and penetrating
eyes. They are coldly
threatening and give
orders for the sighting
to be kept secret. Yet,
strangely, it never is.

*The Men in Black travel in large, black, old-
fashioned cars—maybe a Rolls Royce in the U.K.
or this 1948 Lincoln Continental in the U.S.*

133

Life on other planets

Most people agree that we are unlikely to be alone in the universe. There must be life elsewhere, including intelligent life. It is impossible, however, to predict what these life-forms would look like. We tend to visualize creatures that vaguely resemble us. Yet beings from very distant planets, living in environments that we cannot even guess about, might be unimaginably different. One thing we know for sure is that we are searching.

In 2005 a camera on the European Space Agency probe called Mars Express took clear photographs of a patch of ice within a Martian crater. Mars Express has also discovered signs of ice deep under the surface. This means that life is possible, and, even if Mars is lifeless now, it could have supported life once.

The "face on Mars" is around 1 mi. (1.6km) long and more than 980 ft. (300m) high. Is it a monument created by intelligent life? This picture was transmitted by Viking 2, *which landed on Mars in 1976—though later images suggest that it is only rocks and shadows.*

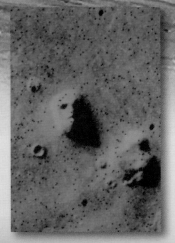

SEARCHING THE GALAXIES

Martians were probably the first extraterrestrials that anyone on Earth thought about. Now that probes have searched the surface of Mars and the possibility of finding intelligent life has diminished, scientists are trying to find life in other galaxies. In 2006 five stars were identified that may have planets with intelligent life orbiting them. Radio telescopes (right) listen and transmit across vast distances and may even reach other planets. They are trying to pick out, from the random sounds of the universe, any that form patterns. They are also transmitting in the hope of reaching distant planets. Maybe the call will be returned one day.

List of Phenomena by Area

Some of the phenomena in this book have occurred in many places. Some, though, are specific to a country or an area. These are listed here.

Africa

Cameroon:

Mokele Mbembe *water monster* (page 75)

Egypt:

Great Pyramid of Cheops *ancient mystery* (page 101)
Great Sphinx *ancient mystery* (page 100)
Tutankhamen's tomb *curse* (page 48)

South Africa:

The Flying Dutchman ghost ship (page 20)

Asia

Shangri-la *lost land* (page 106)
Yeti *land monster* (page 76)

India:

Subbayah Pullavar *levitator* (page 32)

Russian Federation:

Tunguska *fireball, 1927* (page 62)

Tibet:

monks *levitators* (page 64)

Turkey:

5th Territorial Battalion *disappeared in Gallipoli, Turkey, 1915* (page 86)

Australasia

Australia:

bone pointing *curse* (page 48)
Song Lines *spiritual patterns* (page 123)
Yowie *land monster* (page 76)

Europe

Turnfalken *birds of ill omen* (page 51)

Balkans:

Joseph de Lanyi *dreamed the future* (page 28)

France:

Bourges *raining francs, 1957* (page 66)
Carnac *standing stones, ancient mystery* (page 94)
Dieppe *haunted battlefield* (page 16)
Versailles *haunted palace* (page 15)

GLOSSARY

apparitions Ghosts or phantoms.

aura A light believed to surround each living thing; not visible to everybody.

benevolent Friendly, kind, or helpful.

blasphemous Disrespectful toward any sacred being or place.

cataclysm A violent disaster.

covert Secret or concealed.

disembodied Not attached to a body.

DNA Stands for deoxyribonucleic acid, a material found in all living bodies. No one person's DNA is exactly the same as any other's.

doomsday The day of the last judgment by God; the end of the world.

electromagnetic field An area affected by electrical and magnetic forces working together.

elusive Difficult to find.

enlightenment Being in a state to understand a great truth.

evaporates Dries from a liquid form (for example, water) to a vapor (fog or mist).

evil eye A stare or nasty look, believed to be able to cause harm.

extinct Died out and no longer in existence.

extraterrestrials Beings from outside or beyond planet Earth; aliens.

familiars The spirit servants of witches or wizards, often taking the form of cats, hares, or owls.

fissures Long, narrow splits or cracks on the surface of Earth or in rocks or ice.

foreboding A sense that something bad is going to happen.

forensic examination A thorough, scientific, physical examination using various skills, including medicine and chemistry.

genetic experiment Working with the genetic material of living creatures in order to change them. (Genetic material is responsible for everything about an animal or person—appearance, health, etc.)

gravity The force that pulls a body or object toward the Earth.

hallucination Seeing (or possibly hearing) something that is not really there.

hemispheres The northern and southern halves of Earth on both sides of the equator.

heresy Believing something different from the accepted beliefs of a religion or culture.

hoaxes Fakes, imitations of a real thing, tricks, or practical jokes.

illusion A deception or a false belief.

impenetrable Not able to be taken by force.

infrared Below or beyond the red part of the spectrum of light. An infrared camera can take photographs in the dark.

intuition The ability to understand something instantly.

long barrows Long, narrow mounds of soil, usually grass-covered, built by Neolithic peoples to bury their dead.

meditation Serious thought or an exercise for the mind with religious or spiritual significance.

mediums People who can (or believe that they can) communicate with the dead and see "spirit bodies" or auras.

meteorites Small pieces of rocks that fall to Earth from space without burning up in the atmosphere.

mummification Preserving the bodies of the dead.

mystics Those who work toward a spiritual understanding of great and mysterious truths.

Neolithic From the Stone Age— 3000 to 1800 B.C.

oath A solemn promise.

omen Something that happens or is seen and is thought to predict the future.

oracles People or objects that can predict the future.

paranormal Something that is beyond normal explanations.

parapsychology The study of paranormal psychology (behavior, characteristics, etc.).

phenomena Plural of phenomenon—a fact or an event, especially if it is thought to be strange or unexplained.

physicists Those who study or are skilled in physics, which is the science of matter and energy.

poltergeists Mischievous, noisy ghosts that can cause objects to move.

prosperity Wealth.

psychic A medium or person with the ability to see beyond the physical world.

resurrection The act of coming back to life after death.

rites Religious or ceremonial acts.

sacred Holy, connected with religion, or possibly dedicated to a god.

sarcophagus A stone coffin.

seismographs Instruments that measure the strength and direction of earthquakes.

shamans People who form a link between this world and the world of gods and spirits. Sometimes a type of priest.

shape-shifters Creatures with the ability to change from one shape into another—a wizard into a dragon or a witch into a hare or cat, for example.

skeptics Those who doubt or question the beliefs of others.

solstices The two times of the year when the Sun is at its highest or lowest point in the sky at noon—the summer solstice is the longest day; the winter solstice is the shortest day.

spectral Ghostlike.

spontaneous Sudden, unplanned.

strafing Attacking with machine-gun fire.

subterranean Below—perhaps deep below—the surface of Earth.

supernatural Outside the normal laws of nature; mystical or magical—for example, ghosts.

taboo Forbidden, to be avoided.

talisman An object with magical powers.

theories Ideas used to explain things.

treason Betraying your country or your leader.

visions Things seen in the imagination or in dreams or in trances.

yogi A dedicated follower of the Hindu system of yoga, which includes exercise and movement, meditation, and self-discipline.

INDEX

Acknowledgments

The publisher would like to thank the following for permission to reproduce their material. Every care has been taken to trace copyright holders. However, if there have been unintentional omissions or failure to trace copyright holders, we apologize and will, if informed, endeavor to make corrections in any future edition.

b = bottom, *c* = center, *l* = left, *r* = right, *t* = top

Cover: *c* Corbis/Zefa/Theowulf Maehl; *t* Getty/Iconica; *inset* Corbis; Pages: 1 Science Photo Library (SPL)/Garion Hutchings; 2–3 Getty Imagebank; 4 Nick Harris/Virgil Pomfret Agency; 5 SPL/David Hardy; 6–7 Corbis/Hulton; 8 Patricia Ludlow/Linden Artists; 9 Francesca Pelizzoli/Virgil Pomfret Agency; 10–11 Topfoto; 12*t* Alamy/Design Pix; 12*br* Topfoto; 13*tl* Topfoto; 14–15 Alamy/Imagestate; 15*t* Corbis/Adam Woolfitt; 15*b* Corbis/Ali Meyer; 16–17 *background* The Art Archive; 17*bl* Corbis; 17*r* Nick Harris/Virgil Pomfret Agency; 18-19*t* xx; 18*b* Alamy/John Foxx; 18*b* inset Alamy/Patrick Ward; 19 Topfoto; 20*t* Bridgeman Art Library (BAL)/Royal Albert Memorial Museum, Exeter; 20–21 Nick Harris/Virgil Pomfret Agency; 22–23 & 24–25 SPL/Sovereign, ISM; 25*br* SPL/Oscar Burriel; 26*l* Alamy/Ace Stock Ltd.; 27*b* Topfoto; 28*cl* Corbis/Bettmann; 28–29*c* Richard Hook/Linden Artists; 29*tc* SPL/Laguna Design; 29*br* Corbis; 30*tr* Topfoto; 30*bl* Topfoto; 31*tr* & 31*cr* SPL/Garion Hutchings; 31*br* Alamy/Giles Angel; 33 Shane Marsh/Linden Artists; 34–35 Patricia Ludlow/Linden Artists; 36*tr* The Art Archive; 36*b* Topfoto; 37 Getty Images; 38*b* Patricia Ludlow/Linden Artists; 38*tr* Corbis; 39*bc* Corbis/Todd Gipstein; 39*cr* Alamy/Blackout Concepts; 40*br* Photolibrary.com; 41*tl* Rex Features; 41*b* Patricia Ludlow/Linden Artists; 42*tl* Getty Imagebank; 42–43 Patricia Ludlow/Linden Artists; 43*tr* SPL/Mehau Kulyk; 43*br* Getty Stone; 44*tr* Corbis; 44*cr* BAL/Smithsonian Institution, Washington; 44*cl* Corbis/Carl & Ann Purcell; 45*tl* Corbis/Tim Graham; 45*b* Patricia Ludlow/Linden Artists; 46*cll* The Art Archive; 46*clr* Werner Forman Archive; 46*br* BAL; 48*tr* Corbis/Richard T. Nowitz; 48*bl* Corbis/Hulton; 49*tr* AKG, London; 49*br* Corbis/Bettmann; 50 Getty/Photographer's Choice; 51*bl* Alamy/Holgar Ehlers; 52–53 Alamy/Kathy Wright; 53*br* Alamy/Blickwinkel; 54–55 *background* Corbis/Jean-Pierre Lescourret; 54*r* The Art Archive; 55*tl* Alamy/Sylvia Cordaiy; 55*tr* Getty/Taxi; 55*br* Patricia Ludlow/Linden Artists; 56*l* Agnes Olsen; 56–57 BAL/V&A; 57 Getty/Stone; 58*bl* Topfoto; 58*cr* Corbis; 59 Francesca Pelizzoli/Virgil Pomfret Agency; 60–61 Frank Lane Picture Agency; 62–63*t* Corbis/Rodney Hyett; 62–63*b* Corbis/Star/Zefa; 62*cl* Topfoto; 64*bl* Nick Harris/Virgil Pomfret Agency; 64–65 Getty/Robert Harding; 66 Photolibrary.com; 66*tr* Getty/Frans Lemmens; 67 Getty/Photodisc Red; 69 Topfoto; 70 Nick Harris/Virgil Pomfret Agency; 71*tr* Topfoto; 71*bl* Topfoto; 72–73 Frank Lane Picture Agency; 74*r* Topfoto; 74*bl* Topfoto; 74–75 Topfoto; 75*r* Topfoto; 76–77 Fortean Picture Library; 78*t* Fortean Picture Library; 78–79 Corbis/Buddy Mays; 79*tr* Natural History Picture Agency; 80–81 Alamy; 82–83*b* Alamy/Popperfoto; 83*cl* Corbis/Bettmann; 84*tl* Getty/Photodisc Green; 86–87*b* Corbis/Hulton; 86–87*t* Northern Lighthouse Board, U.K.; 87*cl* "Mystery of Eilean Mor" by Gary Crew, illustrated by Jeremy Geddes, published by Lothian Books, Australia 2003; 88*bl* Alamy/Popperfoto; 89*tl* Alamy/Dennis Hallinan; 89*br* Alamy/Jeff Morgan; 90–91 GLASTONBURY TOR; 92 Topfoto; 93*t* Birmingham Galleries, Birmingham; 93*br* Cover, Spain; 94–95 Getty/Stone; 95*t* Alamy; 96–97 Alamy/Atmosphere; 97*t* Corbis/Greenhalf; 97*b* Topfoto; 98*tl* Corbis/Sygma; 98–99 Richard Hook/Linden Artists; 99*b* Corbis/Eye Ubiquitous; 100 Getty/Photographer's Choice; 100–101 The Art Archive; 101*tl* Corbis/Vanni Archive; 101*cr* Empics/Associated Press; 102–103 BAL/British Library; 104*tr* Getty Imagebank; 104–105*b* Topfoto; 105*tr* Topfoto; 106–107 BAL/Tretyakov Gallery, Moscow; 107*r* BAL/Museo del Oro, Bogotá; 108–109 Alamy/Diomedia; 110*bl* Corbis/Richard T. Nowitz; 111*tl* Alamy/Imagesource; 112–113 Alamy/Eureka; 114*cl* Alamy/Wildscape; 115*l* Corbis/Reuters; 115*tr* Getty/Photodisc Green; 116*bl* Empics/AP/Anthony Stalcup; 116–117*t* Corbis/Zefa; 117*br* Alamy/Woodystock; 118*cl* Getty Aurora; 118–119*b* Natural History Picture Agency; 119 Alamy/Carol & Mike Werner; 120–121 NASA; 122*c* Alamy/Philip Scalia; 123*tr* Corbis; 124*b* Topfoto; 125*tl* Topfoto; 125*tr* Alamy/Kim Karpeles; 126*cl* Topfoto; 126*br* Topfoto; 127 Corbis/*San Francisco Chronicle*; 128–129 Getty Imagebank; 130*cr* SPL/Victor Habbick Visions; 130*b* Corbis/Reuters; 131 Getty/Hulton; 132 SPL/Mcgrath/Folsom; 132–133*t* SPL/Victor Habbick Visions; 132*br* Getty/Photonica; 132*bc* Getty Stone; 133 Alamy Wend Images; 134*br* SPL/ESA/DLR/FU Berlin(G. Neukum); 135*cr* SPL/NASA; 135*br* SPL/David Nunuk